the
yellow
wallpaper
and other sermons

the yellow

wallpaper
and other sermons

Peter Carnley

Anglican Archbishop of Perth and Primate of Australia

HarperCollins*Publishers*

HarperCollins*Publishers*

First published in Australia in 2001
by HarperCollins*Publishers* Pty Limited
ABN 36 009 913 517
A member of the HarperCollins*Publishers* (Australia) Pty Limited Group
www.harpercollins.com.au

HarperCollins*Publishers*
25 Ryde Road, Pymble, Sydney, NSW 2073, Australia
31 View Road, Glenfield, Auckland 10, New Zealand
77–85 Fulham Palace Road, London, W6 8JB, United Kingdom
Hazelton Lanes, 55 Avenue Road, Suite 2900, Toronto, Ontario M5R 3L2
and 1995 Markham Road, Scarborough, Ontario M1B 5M8, Canada
10 East 53rd Street, New York NY 10022, USA

National Library of Australia Cataloguing-in-Publication data:

Carnley, Peter.
   The yellow wallpaper and other sermons.
   ISBN 1 86371 799 4.
   1. Carnley, Peter, Archbishop – Sermons.
   2. Anglican Church of Australia – Sermons.
   3. Ordination of women – Anglican Church of
   Australia – Sermons. 4. Sermons, English – Australia.
   I. Title.
252.0394

Cover design by Adam Yazxhi, Max Co
Internal design by Luke Causby, HarperCollins Design Studio
Typeset in 10.5/15.5 Stempel Garamond by HarperCollins Design Studio
Printed and bound in Australia by Griffin Press on 79gsm Bulky Paperback White

6 5 4 3 2 1   01 02 03 04

For
Benedict and Louise,
Sarah and Patrick

CONTENTS

PREFACE

On the Feast of St Augustine of Canterbury, 26 May 2001, I shall have been Archbishop of Perth for twenty years. During that long period of time I have preached hundreds and hundreds of sermons. This selection of just thirty-four of them is comprised mostly of occasional sermons. That is to say they are not Sunday sermons preached to a regular congregation and based on the scriptural readings set in the Church's lectionary for the day. Generally speaking they are not therefore expository sermons. Rather, they are, with a few exceptions, sermons preached on special occasions to mark quite specific events. In some cases congregations have been made up, not of regularly worshipping and committed Christian people, but of less regular attendees and fellow travellers. Often the line of approach has been to begin with human experiences and then seek to bring the fundamental truths of the Biblical revelation to bear on them so as to interpret them theologically and thus make religious sense of them. The exegesis of scripture is therefore more often than not implicit rather than explicit.

The sermons have been arranged in the historical sequence

in which they were delivered. They are prefaced with a brief indication of the context of their delivery. They provide an example of the earnest attempt of one Christian to bring the truths of faith to bear on a wide range of events. They may thus have a historical value as a record, if fragmentary, of a twenty-year preaching ministry. Certainly, it has been an interesting exercise for me to look back over the last twenty years and to marvel at the range of events that have invited religious comment.

I do not think this is the kind of book that I would advise people to read in one sitting, from cover to cover. I hope readers may find these sermons spiritually useful, perhaps as bedtime reading, when just a few pages are needed to trigger some reflective thought at the end of the day.

I hope also that this publication may compensate for the disappointment of those many people who have from time to time so generously asked if sermon texts might be made available, but who have, because of the pressures of my other commitments, never actually received them.

I am very grateful to my Chaplain, the Reverend Sean Mullen, who organised the preparation of the manuscript for publication at a busy time of the year, and to Melanie Hare, Amanda Griffiths and Carene Aubertin who all helped type the texts into a computer. Brigid James has brought wonderful copy-editing skills to the simplification of my contorted sentences. My wife Ann is always a supportive and helpful critical listener to my sermons and it will be obvious to readers that she has had an intimate part in the life experience and faith journey reflected in them. I thank her for all that she is and has been for me, especially for her help in the selection of this particular collection and in editing and encouraging the publication.

These sermons are particularly dedicated to my children, Benedict and Sarah, and their partners in marriage, Louise and Patrick, and to all those patient and reflectively attentive souls who have been prepared to listen and to discern the Word of God in and through them.

+ Peter Perth
Archbishop's House, Perth

1

1881 – A Vintage Year

Preached on 25 November 1981 at St Thomas More College in the University of Western Australia, to commemorate the one hundredth anniversary of the birth of Pope John XXIII, ecumenist.

1881 was, by any reckoning, a vintage year. Not only was it the year of birth of the three great Roman Catholic ecumenists of our time – Pope John XXIII, Cardinal Augustin Bea and Father Paul Couturier; it was also the year of birth of Pierre Teilhard de Chardin and William Temple, Archbishop of Canterbury. And just to keep a toehold in the secular world, I should mention that 1881 was also the year of birth of Bela Bartok, P.G. Wodehouse and Pablo Picasso!

Only one of this list, however, was actually born on this very day – John XXIII. It is, of course, particularly fitting that his birth should become the focus for a celebration of the modern flowering of ecumenism within the Roman Catholic Church. There can hardly be any doubt that the Second Vatican Council which he called will stand in the history books as one of the most important events of twentieth century church history, and certainly as a most decisive turning point in the Christian Church's modern pilgrimage towards that full and complete unity for which Christ himself prayed.

All three members of this ecumenical triumvirate have something significant to say to us, first as a group and then as separate individuals.

As a group, they are of significance because, for one thing, they all achieved their really great work quite late in life. Paul Couturier was fifty-one years old before he was seized by the burning desire to work and pray for the unity of Christians, which eventually resulted in the establishment of the Week of Prayer for Christian Unity. Now fifty-one may not seem so old to some of you, but it does to me! Paul Couturier made his great prayerful contribution to Christian unity during the last twenty years of his life. John XXIII was already seventy-eight when elected pope: 'Too old,' many said 'to be anything more than a caretaker.' Cardinal Bea was seventy-nine in 1960 when he emerged at the close of his scholarly career at the Pontifical Biblical Institute to become president of the newly created Secretariat for Christian Unity.

At ages when most of *us* will be thinking of retirement, well prepared to leave it all to another generation, these men made a contribution to the life of the Church of the very greatest significance. That is a parable for all of us.

We all know only too well that the reintegration of the churches is a slow and painstaking work; it is easy simply to project our hope for the eventual full communion of all Christians somewhere in the distant future. It is tempting to say 'probably not in my time; sometime after I'm gone'. But if there is one thing that John XXIII, Cardinal Bea and Paul Couturier have to say to us, it is that great and momentous and significant things can be accomplished in our own time and perhaps quite unexpectedly. We say, 'That will come about in God's good time', by which we mean not now, not in *our* time. But our time scale is not necessarily God's eternity, which has a certain instantaneousness about it, and our ways are not necessarily his way. Perhaps we should all be a little readier for God to do much more with us and through us, ecumenically speaking, than we ever dare or even care to expect – just as he did with the gang of three whom we commemorate tonight.

Paul Couturier laid the foundation of modern ecumenism in prayer, and more than just the annual *week* of prayer for Christian Unity. There is, in his earnest and constant intercession for Christian unity over twenty years, a sustained and underlying foundation of prayerful longing which provides us with a paradigm to emulate. He is a reminder to us that the active ecumenism of coordinated and shared Christian work in the world or the comfortable armchair ecumenism that characterises many an ecumenical study group of a council of churches or bilateral conversation, are both very thin forms of ecumenism unless they are underpinned by an ever-deepening personal commitment to unity. That is achieved only in the quietness of individual contemplation and prayer.

We all have a good deal to learn about the nature of ecumenism from the famous *Decree on Ecumenism* of the Second Vatican Council, but one of its most important points is its emphasis on the need for what might be called the spirituality of ecumenism. It is interesting that an early draft of the decree focused mainly on the return of individuals to the updated Roman Catholic Church, and had very little to say about dialogue, the status of other churches and ecclesial communities, or prayer. But the decree, as adopted on the 21 November 1964, stresses all these things. In particular, it underlines the intimate relationship between Church unity and the eucharist, and speaks of the eucharist both as that which signifies the unity of the Church and as a means by which that unity is brought about.

By speaking of the eucharist both as a sign of unity and as a means by which it is brought about, the decree does not mean that intercommunion should be embraced without further ado, as though other issues that divide us were matters of indifference. Rather, the decree means that for all the good achieved by our dialogue and talking, and the common action that is possible, every eucharist deepens the unity of the Church, a unity which subsists in one degree or another in every Christian community. Even as we worship in our separated denominations, our commitment to each other in our eucharistic celebrations when we commune together with Our Lord present, achieves a deepening unity which is the ground and promise of greater unity to come. Having glimpsed the unity of Christians at each eucharist, we can lift our eyes to the future in hope of a greater all-embracing unity.

Apart from stressing the intimate relationship between the eucharist and Church unity, the Vatican decree also emphasises the need for individual sanctity as a means to unity. A purifying of motives, an emptying of ourselves of vested interests, and the development of a complete openness to whatever may be required of us in the future is essential to true ecumenism. As the decree says, 'there can be no ecumenism worthy of the name without interior conversion'. The unity we seek is no mere outward organisational uniformity or ground plan for cooperation, nor a mere assent to an agreed statement of doctrine with the top of our heads, but a much more fundamental and deep commitment to one another in peace and love.

So that is the first great contribution of the *Decree on Ecumenism* of Vatican II. I call it 'spiritual ecumenism' as against a mere outward or organisational ecumenism or the armchair ecumenism of some discussion groups. This is the strand in modern ecumenism bequeathed to us by Paul Couturier.

As a biblical scholar at the Pontifical Biblical Institute for thirty-five years, Cardinal Bea was able to bring to the Secretariat for Christian Unity a mature and sensitive appreciation of the current theological consensus concerning the nature of the New Testament scriptures and of the biblical truths to be found in them as a result of modern historical criticism. Behind the current ecumenical consensus is the international work of biblical theologians of the last fifty years, engaging in a dispassionate quest for biblical truth which cuts clean across denominational barriers. One writer has spoken of the merging of the German (Lutheran and Reformed) tradition of biblical scholarship and modern Roman Catholic biblical scholarship under the title of *The Rhine flows into the Tiber.* Cardinal Bea brought his own direct experience of that to modern Roman Catholic ecumenism, and I do not think we can underestimate the importance of it.

The advances of modern biblical scholarship that are the common property of all churches are still being made. In some respects even the statements from Vatican II are beginning to appear somewhat dated. For example, twenty years ago when the Council opened, there was a theological debate going on about the relationship between scripture and tradition. The Vatican Council made some headway in clarifying that relationship. But over the last twenty years of biblical scholarship it has become clear that, when the New Testament speaks of revelation, it generally speaks of it as an occurrence, not in the past but in the future. The day of revelation is the day of the Lord when all things will be clearly revealed – Teilhard's omega point.

We are now beginning to see that the insights contained in scripture and the deliverances of tradition are provisional, in the literal sense of 'pro-visional', that is before the vision. Even the full dimensions of the church catholic are yet to be clearly seen; it does not yet appear what we shall be. This means that in our ecumenical work we do not just shuffle around the inheritance of scripture and tradition, but grow together in ever deepening insight as we move towards the truth of the coming great Church. New biblical insights constantly transform our understanding. Cardinal Bea is a shining representative of this input to modern ecumenism.

Given the underpinning of spiritual ecumenism of the Couturier type and the secure biblically based ecumenism of the Bea type, there was still the need for the catalyst to trigger it all off – a charismatic personality, raised up by God to catch a vision and to do just the right thing at the right moment.

In 1980 my wife and I had a very long and splendid seafood lunch in a little restaurant in Venice, which led to a protracted discussion between my wife and the chef about how one cooks seafood to get it just right. He gave her some good tips about the preparation and the cooking. First you do this and then you do that, he said, with much seriousness. 'But there is always one further thing you need,' said my wife to the chef. 'To get it all together at just the right time you need just a little bit of luck.' Our chef was greatly amused by this – and we were lucky enough to be given a bottle of white wine to bring home to Australia!

John XXIII provided just that little bit of luck, which from the perspective of faith we call providence, to make the ecumenically right move at the right time. John XXIII himself spoke of the unpremeditated and spontaneous way in which Vatican II came to be called. And there is just the hint that he may not have fully understood all that was about to be accomplished by that decision, that he did not have a very developed idea of what ecumenism was really about. There are suggestions that he envisaged an updating designed to encourage the return of individual Christians to Rome (as in the first draft of the *Decree on Ecumenism*) rather than a prayerful dialogue with other churches and a growing towards the genuinely new Church of the future. Indeed, there is a celebrated remark in his diary *The Journal of a Soul* that he made when he was working in Istanbul. He looked through his window over the city at night and lamented that there were so few Christians in the city – only Jews and Muslims and Greek Orthodox!

Whatever John XXIII's own understanding of things ecumenical, it is clear enough that his unique contribution provided the little bit of luck needed to trigger off a movement that went well beyond his own intention. A movement that permitted the underpinning of prayer and the solid background of biblical scholarship to come fully into play.

God does not repeat himself when he acts. He distributes individual gifts to particular people, so that the one complements the other in a rich diversity. In Couturier, Bea and John XXIII we certainly have very complementary figures, representing the prayerful underpinning, the firm biblical basis and that little bit of inspirational luck to do the appropriate thing at the right time which constitutes the modern experience of Roman Catholic ecumenism. There is great cause in it for all of us to give thanks. There is a sure ground from which to hope for that full unity in Christ that

God wills. We all have a great deal to learn from Paul Couturier and Augustin Bea. And may we ever be mindful of the fact that, as we celebrate the centenary of the birth of John XXIII, it may be God's plan for us to be much more than mere ecumenical caretakers.

2

WILD GEESE

PREACHED AT CHRIST CHURCH, BRUNSWICK IN THE
ARCHDIOCESE OF MELBOURNE ON 15 JULY 1983 TO MARK THE
150TH ANNIVERSARY OF THE OXFORD MOVEMENT.

I would like you to think of yourselves, just for a few minutes, as geese – I think the correct term would be a 'gaggle of geese'!

We are very familiar with the biblical image of the flock, but usually it is not a flock of birds. Rather it is a flock of sheep, for the Church of God is a flock under a shepherd. That tranquil image warrants a good and useful bit of discourse about the nature of the Church as a gathered community, and about the shepherding nature of her ministry of pastoral care. It also speaks of the protective nature of the episcopal ministry of oversight, which is to defend the sheep from the wolves. But, like all models that we use to conceive of the Church and its nature, that particular model of the shepherd and the sheep does not exhaust all that can be said about the Church and its ministry. Indeed, it can lead us to some quite unfortunate conclusions.

The image of the sheep and the shepherd leads very easily into a rather passive view of the Christian congregation. It suggests that the Church should gather as a trembling, docile and somewhat defenceless group of people, huddling together in the warmest corner of the field, the place where sheep may safely graze! Or it suggests a view of the Church passive in ministry; that the congregation's job is simply to congregate while the priest's role is to shepherd and care for them. That image leads all too easily to what is called the 'lead–follow' syndrome. The people of God are seen at best to be blindly following, or worse, to be treated as though they were frankly dumb and stupid.

It is in order to correct some of these negative associations of the model of the Church as a flock under a shepherd that I invite you to think of yourselves as geese.

We do not often see geese in this country, though I have sometimes seen them when driving through the farmlands of the beautiful south-western corner of Western Australia. In England geese are far more common, of course, and in some parts of the country it is traditional to celebrate the Festival of St Michael and All Angels at the end of September by having a goose for dinner. This is the so-called Michaelmas goose – a cooked goose. That is not the kind of goose I have in mind when I ask you to think of yourselves as geese, though there are times, of course, when we do as individuals get ourselves into predicaments in which we may feel that that image may be entirely appropriate!

Perhaps you are more familiar with the kind of geese that appeared in this country about fifty years ago, made out of china and placed in sets of three on living-room walls – a small one, a middle-sized one and then a larger one, flying together in an ascending line. This image of a line of wild geese evenly placed in a domesticated environment is much closer to what I have in mind as an image of the Church. If the Church is to be thought of as a gaggle of geese, there is an important distinction to be drawn between wild and domesticated geese. I understand that it is very easy for geese to become domesticated. They are content to lose all their natural sense of wild adventure and remain cooped up in a pen or waddling around the farmyard. As a gaggle of catholic-minded wild geese, we must ensure that the life of our Church does not lose the wild sense of adventure that should be a natural part of being a Christian in the world. If I may sustain the image, we should not lose the freshness and vitality of our Christian life and forsake it for the domesticated life of a bunch of old grey legs.

Last century the somewhat eccentric Danish thinker, Soren Kierkegaard, told a little parable about some domesticated geese. They hear a wild goose flying overhead and become excited, for there is a kind of understanding between wild and domesticated geese. However different they are, when the passage of the wild, migrating goose is heard in the air, the domestic geese down on the ground hear it straightaway and, to some extent, understand what it means – liberation, excitement, the adventure of going somewhere. It means discovery rather than domestication, however secure and respectable domestication might be.

And sensing the possibilities of life in the wild, they too begin to flap their wings. But they are heavy old waddlers, thoroughly domesticated and unused to the excitement of adventure. So they beat their wings, cry and fly about in disorderly and unlovely confusion for a while. But they stay close to the ground – and then it is all over.

Christians can be a bit like that. Every now and again we sense the possibilities – for renewal of life, to 'get up and go'.

We get whipped up into an enthusiasm by the latest prophet who flies in from the wild; we get set for adventure and begin to flap our wings. We do not want to be waddlers. We want to move, to migrate to better things, to start a real adventure of renewed spirituality, the adventure into God. But too often we just flap our wings and it all ends in unlovely and disorderly confusion. We do not really go anywhere.

However, if it is hard for tame, domesticated geese to take off, the other side of the penny is that, once off the ground, it is very easy, I understand, even for the wildest of geese to become domesticated. Let me tell you Kierkegaard's parable of the wild goose.

'Once upon a time there was a wild goose. In autumn, about the migrating time, it noticed some domestic geese. It fell in love with them. It seemed a sin to fly away from them, it hoped to win them for its life, so that they would resolve to accompany it when the migration began.

To this end it took up with them in every possible way. It tried to attract them to rise a little higher, always a little higher in their flight that they might, if at all possible, take part in the migration, released from the miserable and mediocre life of waddling around on the earth as respectable domestic geese. At first the domestic geese thought it was quite amusing, and they developed an affection for the wild goose. But soon they got tired of it, they rebuffed it with rough words, chiding it for a fantastic fool without experience or wisdom. But alas, the wild goose had become so familiar with the domestic geese that they had gradually acquired power over it, their words impressed it – and the end of the story is that the wild goose became a domestic goose ...

If the wild goose's plan is to be approved in any way, then it must above all watch out for one thing – that it keeps itself intact. As soon as it notices that the domestic geese are getting some power over it then away, away with the migrating flock! The true Christian, with the Spirit over him, is as different from the ordinary man as the wild goose from the domestic ones. Christianity teaches just what a man can become in life. So here there is hope that the domestic goose can become a wild goose. Therefore stay with them, with these domestic geese, stay with them and be intent on one thing, to try and win them for the change. But for God's sake take care of one thing. As soon as you notice that the domestic geese begin to get power over you, then away, away with the flock, lest the story should end with your becoming a domestic goose, happy in misery.'

We must beware of the domestication of becoming tame and mediocre Christians.

You may wonder why I have chosen to revive an image of Kierkegaard's on this day when we are commemorating the Assize Sermon of John Keble. Soren Kierkegaard was an exact contemporary of John Keble and in many respects the counterpart in Denmark of Keble in England. If you read Keble's Assize Sermon you will find that, in the first instance, the Oxford Movement which it initiated was a protest against the over-domestication of the Church of England. It was a protest against Whig Liberalism trying to assimilate the Church to the State. This was illustrated by the fact that the Reform Bill, which was being debated at the time, tended to treat the Church as little more than a department of the State. But, more importantly, the initial protest of the Oxford Movement was a protest against a tendency in the life of the Church itself to reduce the vitality of any passionate individual commitment to Christ and of any true and deep spirituality to a mediocre conformity, to the values of respectable, domesticated society.

All this was what, on a national level, amounted in Keble's eyes to 'national apostasy'.

Kierkegaard felt exactly the same way and at the same time about the evangelical, established Lutheran Church of Denmark. The Oxford Movement in its origin was not about the externals of worship but about something that an evangelical Lutheran in Denmark could share – a passionate concern to reject a liberal-minded conformity to the respectable but mediocre life of a tame and over-domesticated Christianity. What Keble and Kierkegaard had in common was a concern to recover the inner integrity of faith, as against outward conformity to the mediocre values of respectable society to which State religion, whether in England or Denmark, had allowed itself to succumb.

If we are to draw any inspiration from the Oxford Movement, we have to ensure, above all else, that we do not become domesticated. God forbid that our Church should become assimilated to the mediocre values of the half-hearted commitments of the secular society we seek to win for the change.

We have to do our work in the world as wild geese, living alongside the domesticated geese. We work in the hope of leading these domesticated geese off on the life of wild adventure into God. But as soon as we feel that our domesticated neighbours are getting power over us, taming us and assimilating us to their world, then it's the right time for catholic renewal. This means the renewal of the inner substance of our commitment, renewal in prayer and in eucharistic devotion, and renewal in the spiritual adventure of exploring ourselves in relation to God, perhaps with a priest as spiritual director and soul friend.

Renewal, of course, does not mean a return to the worn-out religious exercises and methods of the past. The Church's methods often need renewal in the sense of reform and renovation, as much as her people. Many of us were brought up on a strictly pre-Vatican II form of the confessional. As a student at Trinity College, I regularly visited this parish church of Christ Church Brunswick for that purpose. The incumbent at the time was a very gifted and loving pastor. But the method of administering the sacrament of penance in those days was somewhat impersonal, even a little mechanical. Its closeted secrecy and the penitent's anonymity made it somewhat less than warmly human. The forgiveness of a kind of grocery list of sins compiled the night before tended to be understood in a mechanical, legalistic way; absolution was 'pronounced'. It was an impersonal dispensing of the grace of forgiveness if ever there was one.

But now we talk less of 'absolution' and more of 'reconciliation', less of penance and more of encounter with the real presence of Christ the Forgiver. So perhaps we should be open to the possibility of the development of a less formal, mechanical form of repentance, in which there is more dialogue between priest as soul friend and an individual about where he or she is at in the adventure of spiritual growth and development. Perhaps there should be less emphasis on the compilation of a list of actual sins of commission and omission and more discussion of where the difficulties lie in relationships and how they might be overcome. Perhaps there should be less talk of petty sins and more of the feeling of frustration in prayer, or the problem of organising one's time, the experience of the absence of God, and the social pressure to fall into moral evil and how to cope with it. Perhaps there should be an element of dialogue and only then a formal element of reconciliation with Christ, with the declaring of his reconciling love and forgiveness. And above all, perhaps priest and penitent should be humanly bound together by the indissoluble link of friendship and the conviction that they are both sinners, both very humanly working their way along the road to perfection. Then we could think not just of the concelebration of the eucharist, but of the priest and penitent concelebrating the sacrament of the reconciling presence of Christ the Forgiver.

There is another thing that the image of the wild geese can teach us. It is a lesson to be drawn from the fact that the wild geese on the living-room wall fly together and in a line. Perhaps you have seen wild geese or wild ducks flying in V-formation across the sky. I wonder if you have ever asked yourself how it is that wild birds organise themselves in V-formation? That is one of the intriguing mysteries of nature now explained by the research of a group of aero-dynamic engineers in Canada. It has been discovered that, as the wild geese fly in V-formation, the flapping of the wings of each bird gives an uplift to the one before and behind, and it, in turn, receives an uplift from them. This lift creates approximately 70 per cent more forward thrust so that, as a group, the geese can fly much, much further than they can individually. If one goose slips out of the formation and tries to fly on its own, it gives and receives nothing.

One of the fundamental insights of catholic renewal in the life of our Church is the conviction that salvation is found together with others. However important it is for us as individuals to resist the domesticating pressure of the crowd, we learn that on the way of salvation, we are supported and uplifted by others and we, in turn, help to uplift them. By flying in formation we get much further than we could if we were to break formation and go it alone.

To be a wild goose then does not mean breaking formation, leaving the group and doing one's own thing as an individualist. That was the tragedy of Kierkegaard who ended as a solitary individual and died forsaken and alone, rebuffed by the Church he sought to renew. He was an individualist with little appreciation of the value of flying in formation. But Keble started a movement. As children of the Oxford Movement we work together in group formation in the Church to which we belong. We work together with a leader out front to set the direction and establish the rhythm of the flight, but nevertheless with everybody contributing energy to get further ahead.

As we celebrate the birth of the Oxford Movement, let us seek the renewal of our methods as well as of our people. And let us vow to be wild geese, passionately committed to spiritual growth among our respectably domesticated brothers and sisters. May we never allow ourselves to be tamed and domesticated by them, flapping our wings from time to time but destined to go nowhere.

3

JOHN RAMSDEN WOLLASTON: THE SAINT WHO 'EARTHED' CHRISTIANITY IN THE WEST

PREACHED IN THE PRESENCE OF REPRESENTATIVES OF THE ANGLICAN PROVINCE OF WESTERN AUSTRALIA IN ST GEORGE'S CATHEDRAL, PERTH ON 23 FEBRUARY 1984, ON THE OCCASION OF THE SOLEMN PROMULGATION OF JOHN RAMSDEN WOLLASTON AS A LOCAL SAINT AND HERO OF THE ANGLICAN COMMUNION IN ACCORDANCE WITH ANGLICAN PROCEDURES ADOPTED IN RESOLUTION 77–80 OF THE LAMBETH CONFERENCE OF 1958.

'If the Church today is going to achieve any lasting breakthrough, we need more than faith, hope and charity. While avoiding any fatal compromises we must proclaim and live the timeless message of the Gospel in more Australian terms; we must earth our religion in this 'wide, brown land'; we must identify more closely with what is good and worthwhile in the Australian ethos, we must sing Australian songs, tell Australian stories and search for Australian saints;

we must see Christ as our own sunburnt Saviour through distinctly Australian eyes', said Alan Grocott in the *Zadok Centre News* for July 1982.

John Ramsden Wollaston, though an Englishman by birth, provides for us an example of an Australian saint who 'earthed' the Christian religion in this wide brown land. By any reckoning Wollaston was a exceptional man indeed, with a very highly developed sense of the providential outworking of the Spirit of God in his life. He possessed a simple but robust faith coupled with a self-effacing humility and an unwavering commitment to the task to which he believed he was called by God.

At the age of fifty, when some today are beginning to think of retirement, he arrived on these shores to commence the work of which we are the direct inheritors. Like many of the early European settlers, his first impression was one of an inhospitable, harsh land of the 'most sombre, uniform hue imaginable'.

He failed to notice the rich variety in the Australian bush, being overwhelmed by one uniform colour, 'a dark, dirty green'. 'I have been almost tempted to shed tears at the desolateness of the scene', he wrote, 'had I not called to mind the ubiquity of the God of Nature who can make a wilderness like Eden, and a desert like the Garden of the Lord.'

The state of religion was hardly more encouraging. Between 1829 and John Wollaston's arrival in 1841 religion among the settlers had 'sunk to a miserably low ebb', as he put it, while all around were 'heathen tribes who had yet to hear the Gospel'.

It was through the instrumentality of John Wollaston himself that God was able to transform that unpromising and desolate scene. At Easter 1842 he had no communicants except members of his own family. On Trinity Sunday of the same year he was cheered by a good congregation of twenty-six plus eight communicants.

Through his labours he not only planted our Church but then ordered its life as Archdeacon of Western Australia from 1849 to 1856 and it was Wollaston who drew the colonial clergy together to take the first initiatives for the appointment of a bishop. Whatever we are and whatever we do today as a province is inseparable from what he was and what he did.

The historical outline of John Wollaston's heroic ministry and the quality of his faith and spirituality can readily be picked up from his journals, along with the many fascinating asides that add both human warmth and charm.

I find myself wondering what the outcome was when Wollaston made his own false teeth, and I note that we must credit him with the production of Western Australia's first water bed. When caring for a parishioner who was dying and in great pain he filled a horse trough with water and stretched a mackintosh across it so that she could rest comfortably. This means, though modern manufacturers do not know it, that waterbeds should carry an Anglican patent!

To speak of John Wollaston and ecumenism is immediately to slip into an anachronism for the nineteenth century was anything but ecumenical. John Wollaston was, of course, a man of his time and at first sight he may seem to be somewhat unecumenical in outlook. He had grave doubts about Quakerism. He could not see the irenic and quietist movement in search of world peace that we know today but rather a very dubious expression of Christian discipleship lacking a commitment to regular discipline. He therefore tended to equate Quakerism with apathy and indifference.

Nor did he seem to have been very welcoming to Roman Catholics as they arrived in the Swan River colony. He had difficulty comprehending how it was appropriate for it to establish an ecclesiastical hierarchy in a British colony. The development of the Roman Catholic Church in Western Australia coincided, more or less, with the years covered by *The Picton Journal* – the early 1840s. In 1841 the Western Australian European settlement had only been in existence for twelve years. It had a population of some 3400 people, with no more than 300 Roman Catholics.

Generally speaking the Roman Catholics were not wealthy nor in possession of farm land but rather labourers or members of the 51st Regiment which was based in the Swan River colony. The first Roman Catholic priest, a Father Brady, was sent from the eastern states in 1843 by the Roman Catholic Archbishop of Sydney, Archbishop Polding. Without Archbishop Polding's permission, Father Brady took himself to Rome in 1844 and reported that there were five thousand Europeans in the colony and two million Aboriginals awaiting salvation.

The Vatican was so impressed that, without Archbishop Polding being consulted, it created a Diocese of Perth and consecrated Father Brady as a bishop. Bishop Brady recruited six priests including the famous Joseph Serra and Rosendo Salvado of New Norcia and six Sisters of Mercy in Dublin. He did this by describing the desperate need for education in the colony, particularly among female European children, and by providing an impassioned description of the neglected state of the Aboriginals.

When the twelve missionaries arrived with Brady as bishop, the governor, Lieutenant Colonel Andrew Clarke who was a devout Anglican, was astonished at the arrival of such a large contingent for such a small Roman Catholic population. And even the sisters were startled to find that their school opened with only six pupils. Mother Ursula Freyne very innocently asked Bishop Brady where the 4000 children were and received the answer that 'out of these stones Almighty God could raise up children to Abraham'.

The arrival of such a large missionary band naturally aroused fears about proselytising and to Anglican eyes it was unthinkable that Roman Catholic clergy and religious could minister outside their own flock. It is clear that John Wollaston felt that a Roman Catholic mission in a British colony was as out of place as an Anglican Mission would have been in Italy.

Nevertheless, contact with members of other Christian denominations was inevitable, especially in a numerically small community, and something of the impact of the Gospel on a man's life can be measured by the manner in which he handled these contacts.

One of the Sisters of Mercy who arrived with Bishop Brady wrote home that 'the respectable people, as they call themselves are, with one solitary exception, Protestants'. The one solitary exception referred to here was Thomas Little and his wife who ran a horse-breeding property called Belvedere on the northern end of Leschenault Estuary.

A Roman Catholic landowner was a rarity and this is reflected in the somewhat surprised remark of John Wollaston himself that, 'though papists, the Littles were very nice people'. A very close friendship developed between the Wollastons and the Littles which, in a sense, transcended the denominational barrier. We find in Wollaston's journal, for example, an occasion when he had killed and dressed a chicken in order to entertain the Littles for lunch. He sent mail with the Littles to India, the Littles gave him a bottle of port and Mrs Wollaston presented a pair of shoes to Mrs Little, who returned the compliment with a turkey.

They were thus very close in human terms even if John Wollaston himself remained firmly convinced of the errors of the papacy. 'I am sorry he is a Romanist', he wrote, 'he and his wife are such nice people and kind neighbours.'

And indeed he wrestled with the agony of Christian division. 'The Littles are such excellent, benevolent people and I regret every time I see them more and more that they are papists. He is certainly one of the most liberal minded of that Church I ever met with.' It's clear that this meeting of two Christians of different persuasions was full of the warmth of the Spirit of God. Scoring points or plain proselytism was unthinkable. John Wollaston was clear about his own views, yet accepting of those who thought otherwise.

In 1982 I was interested to receive a letter from Eileen Mountford of Bunbury who said that one of her forbears, William Moriarty, an Irish Roman Catholic, had married in the early days of the colony but the registration of the marriage could never be located. However, she found it in the records of John Wollaston's services just after the opening of his little church at Picton. Indeed, the first wedding in the new church was between two Roman Catholics on 29 January 1843. Mrs Mountford wrote, 'I wonder, if I had built that church, with all the sacrifice involved, would I have let an Irish papist, with the name of Moriarty, use it first?'

John Wollaston performed the ceremony himself and thus provides us with an early model, not only for the shared use of churches, but for an Anglican to celebrate the marriage of two Roman Catholics which, as an ecumenical act, must rank well ahead of what we are able to do even today!

John Wollaston's dealing with the Aboriginal population makes it clear, once again, that he worked under the limitations of nineteenth century mentality with all its paternalism. For

John Wollaston, the Aboriginals were benign 'savages and heathen', awaiting the arrival of superior European civilisation.

He had heard rumours of cannibalism inland but, generally speaking, when he used the term 'savage' he meant what we mean when we use the term 'native'. His compassion for the poor folk he had fallen in with, to whom he gave some Indian corn, and his clear perception of their gifts is quite unmistakable. His references to Aboriginals are almost always positive and complimentary.

'Black servants are generally good cooks', and he lamented that his present black servant who 'was paid the very high wage of four pounds per year' could not be kept for long at that high rate of pay. 'He has many faults', said John Wollaston, 'though an excellent clever servant if he chooses.'

He also discerned in Aboriginals a certain dignity, 'They are never awkward, shy or confused', and he very early recognised that the white settlers were at fault in giving them liquor. 'I think the conduct of the whites here, considering their advantages, ten times worse than anything the poor savage, under his heathen darkness, can do.'

Among those singled out by John Wollaston for their inhumanity to the Aboriginals was Charles Bussell, who had killed an Aborigine for allegedly robbing him of flour. Bussell pursued the Aborigine to a swamp, and after calling on him to 'stand in the name of the Queen', shot him. 'Most unjustifiable homicide in my opinion', wrote John Wollaston, 'what can a poor savage know about standing in the Queen's name?'

In another incident the same Charles Bussell is said to have killed a little native girl after 'most inconsiderately threatening her'. Her crime was that she was caught with a damper – apparently made out of Bussell's flour. John Wollaston found even the threatening 'perfectly illegal and unjustifiable' and was glad to see Bussell summoned to Perth to be investigated. He found the killing of Aboriginals 'distressing and lamentable'.

While calling for justice for Aboriginals he felt that the education of the natives was the best help he could personally give them and at one point he proposed that Rottnest Island would better be used as a native school rather than as a prison if Aboriginals were going to gain employment opportunities.

In his ministry, he himself claimed to be 'on good terms with them all', his only anxiety being that they might mistake his helping deeds as a form of wizardry. All the while, his compassion and sense of social justice shines through.

Today we are able to see a little further than John Wollaston. We recognise his own human limitations and his conditioning by the age of which he was part. But the saints of God are like that. They are real people and not the simpering, picture book characters we so often see in stained glass windows. We call them saints because we see the life of Christ defined in their lives. We see it shining through their human limitations. And indeed, it is their human frailty that resonates with our common humanity just as their Christ-like devotion is an example for us to follow.

Of course, we cannot just repeat what John Wollaston said and did – his day is not ours. But if we claim to see a little further than he did, we do so only because we stand on his shoulders. His story is part of our story and our province quite simply would not be as it is today without the foundation he laid.

We give thanks to God for him. Our hope is that with history as our judge in a century or so's time, our contribution to modern ecumenism or Aboriginal affairs or any of a hundred other crucial issues will not be found wanting, and that we, too, may be numbered among the saints of God.

4

ON NOT LOSING
ONE'S HEAD

PREACHED IN ST GEORGE'S CATHEDRAL, PERTH IN THE PRESENCE
OF THE WESTERN AUSTRALIAN COMMANDERY OF ST JOHN OF
JERUSALEM, 5 JULY 1987, TO CELEBRATE THE FEAST OF ST JOHN
THE BAPTIST.

In the evening of 2 June 1987 I found myself in one of those extraordinary situations which imprints itself very clearly in one's mind. Indeed, I remember it well because of the element of the bizarre surrounding it.

I was standing in a room in the undercroft of the Chapter House at Westminster Abbey where the general public is not normally admitted. And I found myself looking down at a row of human heads, lying on the floor at my feet. Some of these heads were medieval heads, so you will understand that they were a little the worse for wear; others were in comparatively good condition. Among the most impressive of them was the head of King Henry VII, almost perfectly preserved with barely a blemish on its pale skin, though it was admittedly bald and therefore looked somewhat forlorn.

Now, you will be pleased to know that these heads were carved from wood, some quite exquisitely, and very delicately painted. They were originally parts of fully dressed effigies that lay on the coffin during the funeral ceremonies of the famous persons concerned.

From the Elizabethan period onwards fully clothed wax effigies stood beside the relevant tombs as very life-like reminders of how the great had been in life. And these too, including a really splendid Charles II, now form part of a new and permanent exhibition of the Westminster Abbey effigies.

The strange and sober feeling with which one is possessed as one looks down at the head of the funeral effigy of Henry VII is not to be compared, however, with the shock and surprise that must surely have run through the minds of those present when (according to legend) John the Baptist's head was carried on a platter and presented to Herod's daughter. For us, this kind of thing just does not happen at dinner parties. It strikes us as repulsive; indeed, quite uncouth. We congratulate ourselves that civilisation and good taste have delivered us from having to contend with such occurrences.

When you think about it, even those famous incidents of more recent history in which the great have lost their heads, are far removed from our contemporary experience. I think of those poignant moments when Charles I said goodbye to his wife, and uttered words of pious encouragement to his small children before stepping through the window on to the scaffold to be beheaded at Whitehall. Or when, at Fotheringhay, the executioner held aloft the severed head of Mary Queen of Scots crying out 'God save the Queen'. And, as he did so, the auburn tresses in his hand came apart from the skull and the head itself fell to the ground. The dignified Queen of Scots had chosen to wear a wig for her execution – her own hair had been quite grey.

We hear such stories with a shudder ... and a sense of relief. For us, talk of people 'losing their heads' is, of course, metaphorical talk. Today 'heads roll' only when, because of gross incompetence, it becomes necessary to make quite dramatic changes of personnel.

We speak of 'losing our heads' when, at a department store's end-of-year sale, we come home with a whole lot of ill-fitting clothing that we did not really intend to buy and do not really want or with a ten-year supply of toilet tissue and have no place to store it. To 'lose our heads' today is to act against our better judgment; when prudence and the exercise of reason evade us. We realise we have temporarily lost our heads when we are plunged into what is termed 'buyers' remorse'.

Now, we may think that we live in a far more refined and civilised world than that in which men and women *literally* lost their heads, but I suspect that this may be something of an illusion. It may be that our capacity to be humanly uncouth has just altered the outward forms in which it manifests itself. Indeed it may be that we are approaching one of those periods in human history when a fundamental anxiety tends to take hold of humanity corporately, leading people to lose their heads, make bad judgments and accept questionable values.

Towards the end of the first millennium people began to feel uneasy because they thought that in the year AD 1000 the world would end. The approach of the year 2000 seems to have triggered something similar. The air we breathe is troubled, though not because of millennial fear alone, but for a set of quite concrete and identifiable reasons.

First there is the secular apocalypticism of the nuclear age which regularly makes the international world somewhat nervy.

Recently, after leaving London, I was in southern Wales for the purpose of connecting up a Welsh parish in a sister relationship with one of our own. In the course of a very pleasant civic dinner hosted by the Mayor and Council members of the Borough of Islwyn in the County of Gwent, it became clear that the conversation was going to centre that night around the continuing problem of radioactive fallout from the Chernobyl disaster. This was because the fallout had affected the sheep-farming districts of northern Wales particularly acutely. In the year after Chernobyl no Welsh lamb could be sold because of the problem of radioactivity. It was thought that in the course of time it would diminish in intensity and disperse. What happened, however, was that radioactive rain had gone into the ground and come up again through the grass, which in turn had been eaten by the sheep. Two years after Chernobyl the levels of radioactivity were in fact greater than they were in the first year.

As it turned out, lamb was served at this particular dinner! Somebody suggested that the lights should be turned out to see if it glowed. At the other end of the table I heard a man wondering aloud if his dinner would go 'click, click, click' if a geiger counter were held over it.

The Welsh sense of humour covered a fundamental anxiety which later became more seriously apparent when a lady explained to me that there were seven nuclear power stations on the nearby estuary of the River Severn, and that even if nuclear weapons were eliminated people were still worried because a conventional bomb dropped on one of those power stations would have precisely the same effect as Chernobyl. Perhaps we should expect a growing world anxiety concerning the future of this planet. The question this poses for us is: Will we lose our heads? Can our corporate human judgment under this pressure remain sound?

A second stimulus to the growth of a pervasive sense of apocalyptic concern and anxiety is, of course, the disastrous spread of HIV/AIDS and its increasing incidence beyond a particular sector of our society. The thought that possibly one in ten Americans, and significantly far greater numbers of Africans, will be carrying the virus in the coming decade and that we have hardly begun to face the implications some years hence for those who are already antibody positive, makes us shudder.

And the question is: Do we have it in us not to lose our nerve, to keep our cool and, with courage and balanced judgment, quietly work for the renewal of humankind? Or will we lose our heads, give way to all kinds of ill-founded phobias, over-react with a frightening return to a rigid, repressive and anti-human puritanism or worse with a vindictiveness of a most uncouth and vicious kind?

It has been said that one of the chief causes of the decline of the Roman Empire and the rapid descent of a civilised and stable world into barbarism was a fundamental loss of nerve. A basic human anxiety stifled reasoned judgment and social confidence to the point where an uncouth and uncontrolled self-interest became a predominant force of social and political disintegration.

The tendency towards apocalyptic thought, never far away in times of war, rumours of war, natural disaster or uncontrolled disease, is one form of the melodramatic imagination that exaggerates the darkness of things and overplays the good. Such a contrast between good and evil can be drawn that people, out of anxiety and fear, opt for the simplistic remedy or the all too easy way out.

In religion the modern phenomenon of the charismatic movement among contemporary Christians exhibits some clear signs of the melodrama of the apocalyptic mentality. It shows in an excess of religious enthusiasm that opts out of social concern into a ghetto of individualistic piety with a concentration of interest on a God of extraordinary signs and wonders, and a corresponding harsh judgmentalism on all that belongs to 'this world'. The effervescence of creation science in Queensland and resurgent Muslim and Hindu fundamentalism may be examples of the same kind of phenomenon.

The melodramatic face of apocalyptic thought leads quickly to a devaluing of natural reason; all this is a sign of religion beginning to lose its head.

In the secular realm, contemporary anti-nuclear and pro-nuclear groups likewise tend to see things in terms that are far too simplistic to go unchallenged. The Welsh lady who pointed out that a conventional bomb strategically placed could be just as destructive as a nuclear weapon was surely right. But very curiously, in her concern about the harmful side-effects of the generation of nuclear energy, she seemed quite unaware of the fact that the continued use of solid fuel and its predicted greenhouse effect will also lead to quite horrific consequences. Any negative implications of uranium mining must also be balanced by the long history of tragedy attached to coal mining over the last one hundred years. The folk memory of one Welsh village tells of a fire in a mine that the management dealt with by diverting the local canal into the mine. Three hundred and eighty-six miners were drowned in the process. 'Better to drown,' the management said, 'than to burn'.

Moral issues are never quite as black and white as they are sometimes assumed to be by those who inhabit an all too melodramatic and apocalyptic environment of thought. Humanity does face some fundamental and pressing problems that do threaten our very survival into the next millennium.

But let us not lose our heads by making over-simplistic and hasty judgments based upon little more than corporate anxiety and fear.

Easier said than done you might say. Certainly, we cannot simply deal with a fundamental sub-conscious human anxiety with the snap of our fingers. We can make a good start, however, by very self-consciously placing ourselves in an environment of faith in a God who is on our side; who by incarnation is already involved in the affairs of *this* world; who promises to lead us into all truth and to provide us with sufficient human resources of love and care to allay our anxiety and open the way for us to think through our problems in a prudent and measured way.

Those in places of leadership in our parishes have a particular responsibility to safeguard the purity and authenticity of religion under the pressure of the age to take short-cuts – to opt for a cheapened version of Christianity that may have a popular appeal but which may be, in fact, a counterfeit product when compared with the genuine article.

There used to be a time when to be a Christian did not mean superficially, if enthusiastically, to clap and sing and promote a shallow, unthinking fundamentalism as a substitute for a mature and developing faith. Rather, it meant to be possessed of faith, hope and love infused in us by grace. But underneath these three theological virtues which are the product of grace, as it were, God has created all of us with a natural capacity to pursue the four cardinal virtues. These are within the grasp of any clear thinking human being because of the natural, but no less God-given, gift of reason or common sense. All of them are virtues of the keeping of one's head: prudence or wise judgment, justice or fair judgment, temperance or restraint, and fortitude or courageous and steadfast commitment.

Under the pressure of the charismatic movement, with its emphasis on extraordinary gifts of healing, or speaking in tongues, we have lost sight of these four cardinal virtues – which are also God's gift to us. These are the virtues for which we must strive as we face our many problems, grapple with very considerable challenges, make our decisions and work for the transformation of the world for good.

5

OUR LADY OF WALSINGHAM

PREACHED AT A PERTH DIOCESAN GATHERING OF MEMBERS OF
THE MOTHERS' UNION ON LADY DAY, 25 MARCH 1988.

In 1969, as I was completing my studies in Cambridge, I was
very tentatively approached by the Dean of St John's
College about the possibility of taking up an appointment as
vicar of a parish in Norfolk.

In England, as you may know, the right of appointment of
parish priests often does not lie with the diocesan bishop or
nomination board; instead, in many cases it lies with the
patron of the parish. Often this is the chief landowner of the
area, whose ancestors may originally have established the
parish church and built it on their own land and endowed the
stipend of a priest to function within it. The rights of
patronage thus pass from landowner to landowner along with
other goods and chattels of the property. And it so happens
that St John's College, Cambridge, being by inheritance a not
inconsiderable landowner, possesses the right of patronage of
some fifty parishes in various parts of England, including this
particular Norfolk parish that had fallen vacant.

The proposal was that my wife and I go to Norfolk to live in a very large and rambling sixteenth century vicarage of Tudor style, with some thirty rooms, and open it up to parties of college students who would come to spend an occasional weekend retreat for the good of their souls.

This parish was the neighbouring parish to Little Walsingham; that was one of its attractions. Students coming to the place could make a pilgrimage to the national Anglican Shrine of Our Lady of Walsingham at the same time.

However, I was already committed to returning to Australia to the Diocese of Bathurst and could not therefore countenance the possibility of going to this particular parish. Another reason for not pursuing the matter was that an occasional ministry to college students and a somewhat sleepy Norfolk parish with only two village churches and less than five hundred inhabitants did not seem to be quite challenging enough at that particular time of life. It seemed more appropriate for a priest nearing his retirement. This seemed to be confirmed by the name of the two villages which together comprised the parish, for they were called Little and Great Snoring! Had it been offered to me now things may have been different.

As it turns out the name 'Snoring' does not relate to the sleepiness of the place. Rather, the name of these villages seems to have been associated with John Snoring (1374–1401) who was, in fact, the prior of the community of Augustinian canons who lived and administered the Walsingham Shrine as a place of national pilgrimage. In the late fourteenth century he tried to transform the Augustinian priory at Walsingham into a fully fledged abbey with himself as the mitred abbot by means of a papal bull of doubtful authenticity. But this move was forcefully and successfully resisted by the King and the Bishop of Norwich, who was a wake-up to Snoring (if I may put it that way). Snoring had already tried (without success) to obtain a papal exemption for Walsingham from episcopal visitation and from paying the medieval equivalent of the dreaded diocesan assessment.

This little incident is but one from the checkered history of the Shrine of Our Lady of Walsingham from its foundation in the 1140s to its dissolution in 1538 as part of the reforms of Thomas Cromwell in the reign of Henry VIII, and its re-foundation in 1922 as part of the Catholic revival within Anglicanism in the wake of the nineteenth century Oxford Movement.

The foundation of the Shrine of Our Lady of Walsingham, as you may know, occurred when a noble lady called Richeldis de Faverches, who lived in the manor of Walsingham, reported that she had had a vision of some sort in which the Blessed Virgin Mary appeared to her. In her dream she was transported to Nazareth to the Holy House where the Annunciation, which we celebrate today, had taken place and where the Holy Family had lived during the infancy of Our Lord.

According to the story, Richeldis was commanded to take mental note of the measurements of this house and to make a reproduction of it in England on her own Walsingham land at the site of a certain spring of water.

The resulting shrine, housing a statue of Mary the Mother of the Lord seated on a throne and with the Christ seated in turn upon her knee, enjoyed a measure of importance and popularity as a place of pilgrimage second only to the Shrine of Thomas Becket at Canterbury itself.

In any event, upon the re-foundation of the Shrine in 1922 a replica of the ancient image copied from the medieval seal of the priory was installed as a focus of devotion. There are now replicas around the world, including one in St Boniface Cathedral in Bunbury.

It is appropriate for us to dwell for a moment on its meaning. Why is Mary sitting on a high backed chair-like throne, with her infant Son in turn seated on her left knee? What meaning did that statue have in its own day? In particular, what did those medieval pilgrims think of when they looked upon it and lit a taper before it?

This type of statue, with Mary enthroned and the Christ not so much as a baby but as a diminutive man seated on her lap with right hand lifted in blessing, and both of them in a rather stylised and symmetrical frontal pose rather than a natural or domestic one, was very common through the entire Romanesque period of Church art and into the Gothic period up to the late twelfth century. There are one hundred similar statues from France alone. Clearly, the repetition of the main elements of style points to a commonly held meaning.

According to authorities in religious art and iconography, the throne is not a heavenly throne but a symbolic representation of the throne of Solomon. It is the seat of wisdom, in Latin *Sedes sapientiae*. In the Old Testament it was understood that the wisdom of God could be glimpsed in the order of the universe. The wisdom of God could also be seen in the good order of a harmonious and just human society and in peaceful and harmonious family relationships.

Indeed, in the Old Testament that body of literature called the Wisdom literature – *Job*, *Proverbs*, the *Psalms*, *Ecclesiastes* – emphasises the good ordering of a prudent and moral life. The way of wisdom and prudence was understood to be a godly way of life because it reflected something of the goodness and moral purity and peacefulness of the divine. It was an aspect of the divine that was exhibited by King

Solomon in his good and wise, prudent and considered dispensation of justice.

It is this idea, then, of the Divine Wisdom that is associated with the throne of the statue at Walsingham. And that aspect of the divine is seen also, now in its most complete or definitive revelation, in Christ himself enthroned on Mary's knee. 'Christ', says Paul, is both the 'power and wisdom of God' (*1 Corinthians* 1:24), the tough and the gentle of God perfectly integrated. And he goes on to say that as Christians 'we impart a secret or hidden wisdom of God, which God decreed before all time for our justification' (*1 Corinthians* 2:7); 'that through Christ the manifold wisdom of God might be made known' (*Ephesians* 3:10).

So Christ is the incarnation of the wisdom of God for the purpose of achieving, by his teaching and example, the right ordering and moral goodness of our lives and the making right or justification of the world in justice and peace. And that is perhaps why the child of Walsingham is not a vulnerable little baby passively asleep in his mother's arms, as in many images of Virgin and Child, so much as an alert, intelligent and thoughtful personality, almost a diminutive man. We may note that he even carries a book under his arm. He is the incarnate representation of the wisdom of God, actively conferring the blessings of moral goodness, justice and peace on the world.

And, significantly, he sits dispensing justice while sitting on his mother's knee, so that her knee becomes the throne for the incarnation of the wisdom of God in Christ, who is the source of the good ordering and moral redemption of our lives and of the world. In other words, the mother of the Lord occupies a place between the Old Testament seat of wisdom, Solomon's throne, and Christ the complete or perfect incarnation of the wisdom of God. This is not just another image of Virgin and

Child, but the image of the mother of the Lord and the Incarnate Logos or Word or wisdom of God.

Mary, if you like, is the link between the Old Testament and the New. More particularly she is the feminine link between the feminine idea of the moral purity or wisdom of God symbolised by the throne of wisdom and its incarnation in Christ himself.

The message of the Walsingham statue can thus be crystallised in the phrase 'enseated wisdom'. And when a medieval Christian lit a candle in front of 'enseated wisdom' that was what flooded into his or her mind. Thus in Advent on the 16 December, as we prepare for the Incarnation, we sing the Advent antiphon 'O, *Sapientia*, O, Wisdom':

> Who ord'rest all things mightily:
> Come thou wisdom from on high
> To us the path of knowledge show,
> and teach us in your ways to go.

Hymn 734 in *The English Hymnal*, 'O, *Sapientia*', expresses essentially the same thought:

> O wisdom, which camest out of the mouth of the most high,
> and reachest from one end to another, mightily and sweetly
> ordering all things: Come
> and teach us thy way of prudence.

Now the iconography of our Lady of Walsingham can make a distinctively Anglican contribution to the Roman Catholic celebration of this Marian year and it is important in that ecumenical context. But what does this talk of the incarnation of wisdom have to do with the Mothers' Union and particularly with the Mother's Union study theme for 1988, 'On the Edge'?

Well, I think it may be this. Women have been telling us, and telling us loud and clear, that generally speaking what they have to offer society has not been appreciated and that they have been pushed from the centre to the edges of things. Until our own century women were, by and large, excluded from the decision-making processes of society by the denial of the right to vote. It has only been in our own day that women have been able to pursue interests and careers that formerly were designated 'for men only'.

It would be very stupid to contest the truth that in patriarchal society women were edged out from the centre to the fringes of things – politically, financially, professionally, commercially, educationally, religiously. Only at the domestic level did they occupy anything like a central place.

Of course, with equal educational opportunity and the ability to control fertility, we see women today making their way back into the centre of things. Indeed, it is probably safe to say that the patriarchal age is over. But the danger is that, in this contemporary movement of women from the edges to the centre, there will be a tendency for some, perhaps many women, to begin to operate like men – in that loud, pushy aggressively macho way that we associate with the masculine stereotype.

There is therefore a need for women not to abandon their quest for freedom from the straitjacket of former feminine stereotyping, or to abandon their quest for social justice and the recognition of their worth, but to pursue those goals without losing those unique qualities that we associate with the wisdom of God. For these feminine qualities are qualities which women can bring to business life and to the relationships of men. Women can teach us all the way of prudence, quiet reflection, moral order, harmony, and caring judgment in personal relationships, not just in families but in society at large. Indeed, the incarnation of the Divine Wisdom in Christ reminds us that men and women alike may profitably be transformed and indeed perfected by such values.

As women move, in our society, from the edges to the centre of things, Christian women in particular have a vocation to encourage others to bring with them all those qualities that we tend to learn, not so much from our father's, but at our mother's knee, and that by custom we have traditionally tended to associate more with women than with men: the quietly harmonising influence in a family, prudent and wise judgment and the good order of love and care – the Divine Wisdom.

Christian women have a pivotal role in distributing that to us. After all Solomon's humanity was, by the wisdom of God, transformed so that he did not conform to the usual stereotype of the all-powerful and uncouth oriental potentate. The same wisdom is seen as the perfect incarnation of the divine nature in the image of the Christ, alert, calm and wise, sitting on his mother's knee. And in between the throne of Solomon of the old covenant and the Christ of the new covenant is Mary the Mother of the Lord, whose key pivotal role we celebrate this day for she is an example for us all.

6

THE LAST TEMPTATION
OF THE CHURCH

PREACHED AT THE OPENING EUCHARIST OF THE FIRST SITTING OF
THE FORTIETH SYNOD OF THE DIOCESE OF PERTH IN ST GEORGE'S
CATHEDRAL, PERTH 14 OCTOBER 1988.

In England, at the end of 1865, an anonymously published account of the life of Jesus began to create something of a storm. Indeed, for the first half of 1866 a very animated public debate swirled around it, in both the secular and the religious press. By the end of 1866 it had become known that the author of this controversial work was John Robert Seeley, Professor of Latin at University College, London.

Seeley, who was a devout Christian, called his book *Ecce Homo*. The title is a Latin phrase taken from Pilate's unwitting testimony to the significance of Jesus' humanity when he presented Jesus to the crowd at his trial and said 'Behold the man.' *Ecce Homo*: Behold the man!

As the title suggests, in his book Seeley attempted to explore the humanity of Jesus. He imaginatively looked back to the historical Jesus of first century Palestine and asked: What kind of man are you?

His strategy in writing was to do full justice to Jesus' humanity by postponing any treatment of the divinity.

It was not that he did not believe in the superhuman feats or miracles of Jesus, the Transfiguration or the Resurrection or the Ascension or any other evidence of his divine identity; but he recognised that assent to these aspects of Christ's person and work required a pre-existing faith in God. He sought to address a wider audience and therefore determined to write an account of Jesus whose moral goodness could be perceived by anybody – anybody, that is, who was prepared to think seriously about the mysterious grandeur of Jesus' uniquely significant and compelling life.

Seeley's book drew a wide range of responses. Many were inspired and helped by it; others were perplexed. Still others were offended and outraged by it. The evangelical Lord Shaftesbury described it as 'the most pestilential book ever vomited from the jaws of hell!' Naturally, everybody wanted to get their hands on a copy to read it and this ensured its commercial success!

In the first four months it went through four editions and sold eight thousand copies, with new editions appearing every other year for the next twenty years, until 1888. There could be nothing better to help the sales than a little controversy, unwittingly stirred up by those well-meaning but confused souls who really intended to urge that the book should not be read at all! Later Lord Shaftesbury regretted his remark and even tried to persuade himself that he did not say it.

What then was the problem?

Well, in his attempt to explore the humanity of Christ and present Jesus in a purely human and historical but nontheological way, Seeley suggested that because Jesus was a man like any other normal human being, he had perfectly ordinary human thoughts and feelings about sexuality. It is amusing across the interval of one hundred and twenty years to observe the prim mid-Victorian horror of the reviewers at this shocking thought.

For example, Seeley made the delicate suggestion that, confronted by the woman taken in adultery, Jesus looked to the ground through embarrassment. This provoked the following response from one reviewer, 'The coarseness and latitude of the interpretation was never, we believe, exceeded by any comment which was not designed to be profane'.

That Jesus might have blushed when a woman washed his feet and wiped them with her hair would, of course, have been at the time quite unthinkable.

Another anonymous pamphleteer who complained of the 'indecorous, not to say indecent, mode of writing about our Blessed Saviour' was reduced to speechlessness by some apparently innocuous words that Seeley wrote in connection with Mary Magdalene. 'It is commonly by love itself,' he wrote, 'that men learn the sacredness of love. Yet, though Christ never entered the realm of sexual love, this sacredness seems to have been felt by him far more deeply than by other men.'

The humanly human Jesus portrayed in the book created a furore because it somehow upset the received image of Jesus of much Church piety. Hitherto, Jesus' humanity had tended to be portrayed as a humanity from which sexuality, including sexual thoughts and impulses, had been entirely subtracted. He was somehow sexless.

Now, I suspect you may be entertaining a certain sense of *déjà vu*, for the same kind of belief seems to lurk within the recent wave of negative comment about Martin Scorsese's film *The Last Temptation of Christ*. For many, it cannot even be imagined that Jesus could have been open to sexual temptation.

The controversy unwittingly kicked up by some fundamentalist groups in defending what they believe to be a Christian position created a public interest in the film which it simply does not deserve. In fact, it is a long, slow-moving and third-rate film, entirely lacking in subtlety. I could not in all honesty encourage anybody to bother to go and see it.

However, if there is one redeeming feature of the film, it flows from the genuine attempt of Nikos Kazantzakis, the author of the original novel, to explore the humanity of Christ and particularly the way body and soul, flesh and spirit go together in actual human experience.

The film does not pretend to be a life of Jesus based upon the Gospels. That is made clear at the outset. Rather it is a purely imaginative exploration of how true humanity and the spiritual demands of God's calling to other-worldly vocation might be resolved.

The agony of Gethsemene in which Jesus wrestles about whether to do his Father's will or to go his own way, whether to stay true to his commitment to self-giving love or, at the urging of a cinematic Judas, resort to force and seek a way of escape, is stretched out for the entire two hours and forty-four minutes of the film.

The last temptation is the temptation to come down from the Cross to accept the comfortable human option portrayed in the notorious *imaginary* sequence in which Jesus submits to human sexual temptation, eventually settles down to family life in a quaint country cottage and lives to old age. But in the end Jesus remains true to his Father's will and his own commitment to self-sacrifice. He rejects this last temptation and remains upon the Cross to suffer the agony of a terrible death.

The final outcome is thus the triumph of spirit over the temptation of the flesh to live a normal human life as a family man and this is why the film cannot really be regarded as blasphemous. The film's presentation of the real Jesus, as distinct from the make-believe Jesus of the unlived life that he, in fact, rejects, is in the end true to orthodox belief and one wonders what all the fuss has been about.

The real danger facing us right now is not the stark manner in which the last temptation of Christ is presented, so much as the last temptation of the Church, which is the temptation to abandon the doctrinal norm of our holy tradition that Jesus was truly human.

The fact is that the Jesus of orthodox Christian faith was a true man. He was not a different species of being, a phantom visiting this planet from outer space, but a real man, sharing our humanity to the full. He was tempted in every way as we are, yet without sin. Indeed, as the early Fathers of the Church put it, if the humanity he assumed was not really ours, then the humanity he perfected and redeemed was not ours either, and he becomes entirely irrelevant to us.

The constant temptation of the Church is to idealise Jesus and clothe him with the glorious robes of divine majesty so as to obscure his authentic humanity altogether.

In this sense at least, *The Last Temptation of Christ* provides a corrective to the portrayal of Christ by the communist film director Pasolini in his *The Gospel According to St Matthew*. Pasolini showed a Jesus who passed through the midst of this world without entering into any real human relations with anyone. He presented a kind of detached Jesus who changed the lives of everyone he touched, but without giving any indication that he was affected by them in the way that a normal human being might be.

Such a Christ is, in the technical language of theology, a docetic figure, one who only *appears* to be human but is not authentically human at all. Pasolini's film was much acclaimed by many Christians but its tendency to docetism is a heresy.

The orthodox view is that Christ did not just appear to be human; he was truly human. Moreover, in the orthodox doctrine the unity of divinity and humanity in Christ does not result in the diminishing of his humanity but the perfecting of it.

The Incarnation of God in Christ is an authentic integration of matter and spirit, the perfect union of human and divine without the one obliterating or eliminating the other. In this perfect union the human is not at war with the divine but fully integrated with it so as to produce the perfection of wholeness.

Of course, people who are ill at ease with their own sexuality will be challenged by a portrayal of Jesus' sexuality. They can, in fact, be expected to project a hostility at the film that belongs to a battle going on within themselves. They may have yet to learn that the wholesome integration of our sexual nature into our humanity is precisely what the gift of divine grace makes possible.

The lesson for the Church right now is that we should never submit to the temptation to reduce the full humanity of Jesus to a portrayal of him as less than fully human.

We must also be aware of the pitfall of being tempted to perpetuate a split between body and soul or matter and spirit of the kind that has often been expressed by those who have been critical of the film. Let us avoid the temptation, for example, to take the moral high ground on matters of sexual morality in such a way as to lead to the suggestion that sexuality and sin are synonymous, and then to leave the rest of the world exactly as it is.

Those who have been most hostile to the film's suggestion that sexual temptation may have been real for Jesus even if he did not in fact submit to it, seem content to allow all manner of other dehumanising forces expressed in the film to slip by unnoticed. For example, the last temptation of the Church may be to express its moral outrage about a brief and purely imaginary sequence of sexual encounter with Mary Magdalene, when all through the film the real Christ is unwittingly presented as a perfect exemplification of Hitler's myth that Jesus was not a Jew, but the blonde, blue-eyed, Nordic figure of the ideal race of Nazism. In preserving the racial stereotype of the northern European Jesus, Scorsese's Jesus is not at fault for being too human. The problem is that he is not authentically human enough.

Then there is the temptation to focus on the issue of sexuality and to miss the sadism of the film. If there is anything really objectionable about this film it is the degree of violence and its obsession with blood and self-inflicted suffering. It is said that Nikos Kazantzakis, when he visited the Louvre, wore shoes two sizes too small. He did this, he said, because the enjoyment of beauty should not be had at the price of suffering. Even a somewhat masochistic pre-occupation with suffering as a way of subduing the flesh to allow for the triumph of the spirit does not warrant this film's portrayal of humanly degrading and sadistic violence.

The last temptation of the Church may in fact be the temptation to be a sect and not a Church at all. By definition a religious sect adopts a negative attitude in relation to the world. It seeks to withdraw from it rather than engage with it, as though the chief point of religion is to keep oneself unsullied from the world. Jesus did not come to condemn the world, but some of his followers seem committed to over-compensate for this by adopting excessively condemning attitudes.

A Church is motivated by a positive attitude towards the world. It is realistic enough to see that the world is disfigured and fallen. But the good news of the Gospel is that God is nevertheless its creator and that Christ has come into the world to redeem it. God's mission is to perfect and fulfil the world and the Church is called to be part of that divine engagement.

This means that, as a Church, we must not shrink back from the challenges of an imperfect world but engage with them and work for their redemptive transformation. This is what we stand for on behalf of God. We proclaim the good, liberating news, that what God created he created good, including our humanity and the gift of sexuality. It is the perfection, by God's grace, not the obliteration or repression or the censoring out of an aspect of the authentically human that is our good news. That entails our full entry into the world as Church, not our withdrawal from it in the self-righteous manner of a sect. That, indeed, may be a very constant temptation that persistently challenges us all.

7

St Peter and the Primacy

PREACHED AT ST PETER'S CHURCH, VICTORIA PARK
ON THE OCCASION OF THE PATRONAL FESTIVAL
OF THE PARISH, 29 JUNE 1989.

The prominence given in the Gospel records to Simon Peter among the members of the inner circle of Jesus' twelve close disciples is, of course, sometimes exploited by the Church in order to make a political point.

The Roman Catholic Church, for example, has sought to support a series of claims, not only for Peter but also for Rome and its importance as the See of Peter. This has been done by marrying an ancient tradition that St Peter had journeyed to Rome and died the death of a martyr there, with the story that we find in *Matthew* 16, where, after Peter's confession of faith, Jesus is said to have given the keys of the kingdom of heaven to him with the words 'upon this rock I shall build my Church'. This then becomes the foundation for Rome's claim to be the Primatial See of all Christendom.

Furthermore, successive popes have claimed that the 'power of the keys' given to Peter has passed on to them in the manner of a royal succession. This was used as an important piece of propaganda during the struggle for power between the popes and the Holy Roman Emperors in the Middle Ages. Since the Reformation it has become the basis of Rome's claims to primacy of jurisdiction over all other bishops and pastors and, in a certain sense, over the entire flock of Christ today.

Now, let us consider for a moment the two original elements in this marriage of the ancient tradition about Peter's being in Rome with Matthew's account of Peter's receiving the power of the keys of the kingdom of heaven.

First, let us look at the tradition that Peter died in Rome a martyr. For a long time it was believed that St Peter's Basilica in Rome, and particularly the papal altar within it, had been built over the site of Peter's martyrdom. It was with a view to verifying this tradition that Pope Pius XII (in the pontificate before that of John XXIII) initiated an archaeological examination of the area under St Peter's. This has now gone more or less as far as it can go without endangering the building, and it is now possible to go down below the crypt to inspect the impressive remains.

The archaeologists have uncovered not a Roman circus of the kind where one would expect a martyrdom to have taken place, but rather a pagan burial ground of the first and second century. It consists of rows of family burial chambers, about twelve feet by twelve feet square, separated by narrow pathways and containing niches for urns holding the ashes of the dead. These are clearly pagan for at that time Christians did not cremate.

These mausoleums are by and large intact, except for the roofs which have been, almost without exception, broken off. This is now explained as the work of the Emperor Constantine who became a Christian around AD 313 and built the first basilica on the Vatican Hill on the site of this pagan burial ground. In his preparation of the site he had it levelled and the tops of the mausoleums on the side of the hill knocked off and filled with earth from a little further up the hill in order to create a flat place for his basilica. It is this earth fill that has been painstakingly taken out by the archaeologists.

It is interesting that one of these family burial chambers bears the inscription of a Roman will that requests that the mortal remains of the man buried there be buried in the burial ground 'near the circus' on Vatican Hill. Clearly, St Peter's is built on a burial ground rather than on the site of a martyrdom.

However, the remains of the circus nearby have now been located. If you look at any picture of St Peter's in Rome you will notice in the middle of St Peter's square is an obelisk – a huge monolith, right in the centre. Originally it stood at the left of St Peter's but Pope Sixtus V had it moved in 1586 to the centre of the new square which was later enclosed by Bernini's circular colonnade. The work of removing the obelisk was carried out by 900 men and 140 horses using forty-four windlasses. It took more than four months to relocate the obelisk without breaking it. The move nearly ended in tragedy when, with superhuman effort the huge stone was gradually being raised into position, it remained stationary for one terrible moment – the ropes were giving way. Dead silence reigned as the pope had ordered, under pain of death, that no one was to utter a sound during this dangerous operation. Then suddenly a sailor from Bordighera dared to break the silence. He cried 'water on the ropes' for he knew that this would tighten and shrink them. As a result he saved the day and from then on Pope Sixtus decreed that, as a sign of gratitude, the palms used at St Peter's on Palm Sunday should come from Bordighera.

In any event, the obelisk was relocated; but the interesting thing is that careful drilling has shown that it originally stood right in the middle of a first century Roman circus, a cigar-shaped circuit for chariot racing, which would have been right next door to and contemporaneous with the earliest tombs in the cemetery that has been uncovered under St Peter's. The likelihood is that Christians were martyred in the circus and then buried in the cemetery nearby, for there are certainly Christian inhumations as well as pagan cremations there.

When we look more closely at the excavations under St Peter's we find that the present papal altar stands over a medieval altar, which in turn stands over the altar of Constantine's original basilica. Under that there is a burial – clearly a burial of some significance. Whether the bones that were found there are actually those of St Peter we cannot now know, although it seems to me that there is a high probability that the tradition of Peter's martyrdom in Rome on Vatican Hill may be true. Certainly, the archaeological evidence supports the tradition rather than destroys its credibility.

What then, do we make of the Gospel evidence that is said to support the contention that Peter enjoyed a certain primacy over the others in the inner circle of the twelve? We must turn to the second basic element in the story and here we run into trouble. *Matthew's Gospel* is certainly sympathetic towards Peter and includes the saying of Jesus about the keys of heaven and Peter being the rock upon which the Church will be built. *Mark's Gospel*, which contains the original tradition upon which Matthew built, does not contain these elements. In fact, it portrays Peter in a much less sympathetic light.

When Jesus taught that he was a lowly messiah, one who was prepared and humble enough to accept suffering and even death on the cross, Mark has Peter say 'this can't happen to you – you are the messiah'. Peter was working with his own conception of the messiah as an all-powerful political figure, rather than a self-effacing lowly one. Jesus makes it clear that Peter is mistaken. 'Get behind me Satan,' he says, 'you think as men think, not as God thinks.' There is no mention of the keys of heaven, no mention of Peter being the foundation rock of the Church. And this Marcan version is certainly the earlier tradition. So Roman claims to the primacy over the Church for Peter and for the See of Rome after him on the basis of Matthew's words, may be somewhat insecure.

However, that is not the end of the story. The Matthean petrine texts about the giving of the keys to Peter are inscribed in large gold letters around the cornice inside St Peter's, along with other Petrine texts such as those from *John's Gospel* containing Jesus' direction to Peter, 'Feed my sheep'. But curiously there is one Petrine text that is missing – and it is today's Gospel, *Luke* 24:13–35. In this reading, after recognising Jesus in the breaking of bread, the travellers to Emmaus hurried back to Jerusalem and find people there confessing, 'Jesus is risen indeed and has appeared to Simon' – that is to say Simon Peter.

While this saying is omitted from the collection of sayings carved into the cornice of St Peter's in Rome it is the very one, it seems to me, that could justify some talk of the primacy of Peter. It suggests that Peter was the first to whom the raised Christ appeared. And this is corroborated in the earliest resurrection tradition we have in *1 Corinthians* 15 where Paul lists the witnesses to the resurrection, apparently in order, in the original tradition which he himself had received. And at the top of the list are the words, '*first* he appeared to Peter, *then* to the twelve'.

In *John's Gospel*, a certain primacy is reserved also for Peter. Although outrun by the other disciple whom Jesus loved and who arrived first at the tomb, Peter is allowed to go in first and 'came to faith'. In the resurrection tradition then, Peter does seem to have a certain primacy as the first to have come to resurrection faith. 'He is risen indeed, and has appeared to Peter.'

So while Roman claims based on *Matthew's Gospel* may be a little insecure, perhaps we can help our Roman brethren along a little, with a little friendly ecumenism, by pointing out that they have missed the more authentic evidence in support of Peter's original primacy and importance in the post-Easter community as the first to have come to resurrection faith. It is perhaps this acknowledged primacy in terms of the original resurrection experience that develops into the more explicit and sympathetic presentation of Peter's primacy by Matthew, perhaps writing as a representative of a community where Peter was revered as a hero.

But, of course, a connection between the Church in Rome and Peter, and Peter's importance as the first of the Resurrection witnesses, is a world removed from the claim that his successors have received a particular commission and authority from Jesus. Certainly, it is worlds and even centuries away from the claim that the successors of Peter in the See of Rome are infallible in their dogmatic and moral pronouncements.

Nevertheless, I think as Anglicans in the future we may find ourselves in sacramental communion with the Church of Rome and in order to achieve that we may be willing to concede that Rome has some claim to primacy among the dioceses of the world, just as we acknowledge the primacy of Canterbury among the dioceses of the Anglican Communion. I suspect that in the future we may see the papacy as a symbol of world-wide unity. We may also acknowledge the pope's prerogative of presiding over world-wide gatherings and councils of the Church, providing his role is not seen in isolation but in collegial communion with other bishops. After all, the See of Rome is in fact the only See which claims to have a universal primacy. As the Agreed Statement on Authority of the Anglican/Roman Catholic International Commission has it, 'It seems appropriate that in any future union a universal primacy ... should be held by that See.'

However, whatever symbolic or functional importance the universal primacy of the See of Peter may have, it pales into insignificance alongside the sacramental unity that we shall, by then, have achieved. And given the hint of Petrine primacy in *Luke's Gospel*, in the story of the return of the disciples from Emmaus to Jerusalem, it is a more important truth that the raised Jesus was known on the way to Emmaus in the breaking and the sharing of the bread. For us, to know him in the same way in our eucharist, along with our Roman Catholic brothers and sisters, sharing together in mutual intercommunion, is the more important matter. We may run from our eucharist, back to Jerusalem as it were, back to our ecclesiastical structures, and acknowledge a certain primacy of Peter and of Peter's successors. But the more glorious thing will be to have experienced the unity and harmony of intercommunion together in the presence of our risen Lord in the breaking and sharing of bread.

8

FLYING HIGH WITH
THE EAGLES

PREACHED AT THE ANNUAL SYNOD EUCHARIST ON
20 SEPTEMBER 1991 IN ST GEORGE'S CATHEDRAL,
PERTH ON THE EVE OF THE AFL GRAND FINAL.

Welcome, everybody, to this first session of our forty-first synod.

Every synod has a life of three sessions. This is the first of a new three-year synod and the 120th annual session of the Synod of the Diocese of Perth since our first in 1871. By Australian standards this is a venerable institution.

However, this is the very first session of the very first Synod of the Diocese of Eagle City! And this is something new. Of this we had advance warning some years ago, when somebody entirely unauthorised abandoned the colours specified by the Garter King of Arms for our diocesan crest – azure and argent, which I take to be blue and silver – and reproduced it on a diocesan tie very appropriately, and probably now for all eternity, in blue and gold. I take this to have been a prophetic sign.

It is also a marvel of foresight that in many, if not most, Anglican churches an eagle lectern has been set up as a totem image of what has so recently broken out among us in the form of eagle fever.

Up until recently, of course, local people have tended to identify with the swan as the outward and visible sign of the predominant local spiritual disposition – the swan, ever so elegant and serene, peacefully and reflectively gliding over smooth water, as to the violin accompaniment of Saint-Saens slow and sedate theme (dare I say signet tune) from the *Carnival of the Animals* ... the swan, the perfect picture of composure.

But now the aggressively scowling and defiant eagle has entirely displaced the serene and stately swans of our better nature. It is the image of the eagle that now generates the local mythology of supremacy and dominance and gives us our current self-identity as we glance with threat in our eyes towards the eastern states and in the direction of Melbourne in particular. That is to say, all of us with the singular exception of Francis Xavier Sheehan whose obsession with Essendon is difficult to cure!

The Bible often refers to the eagle, and when one troubles to look the references up, it is clear that aspects of eagle character have in time past spoken to women and men, not of human rivalry, superiority and dominance over others, but of very profound aspects of their experience of the divine.

Let me draw your attention to three aspects of eagle character as they were perceived in the ancient world, and which still have relevance for our own.

Firstly, the eagle's superior size and strength and the impressive breadth of its wings meant that the eagle could fly higher than any other bird. It was the primordial high-flyer, transcending in altitude the abilities of every other creature and building its nest in very high inaccessible places.

From its uniquely transcendent perspective, it could see broader and further and at the same time it could keep its eagle eye on every detail of life and every minor movement in the world below. Thus, Job observed that:

> The eagle mounts up and makes its nest on high ... it lives on the rock and makes its home in the fastness of the rocky crag. From there it spies the prey; its eyes see it ... from far away.

To see with an all-seeing eye; to observe the world from a transcendental perspective, is to see somewhat as God sees. The word 'transcend' means to climb over or to climb beyond, just as the eagle circles high above the mundane world and goes beyond it.

It is by aligning ourselves with the divine, from the transcendent perspective of God our rock, and seeing as God sees, that we observe with sharpened vision a little more of what is actually going on around us than we would otherwise do. The importance of this for us as the people of God is that this gives us the ability to be a prophetic people.

Some may be content to chirp among the twigs, or at best to skim low in showy fashion across the surface of the waters of the earth, or flit from tree to tree, busily going from one thing to another in life. Others may just sit forlorn 'like a screech owl in the desert or a sparrow upon a house top' as the psalmist says. But our vocation is to transcend our local, mundane environment with all its enticements, and to climb above and out of our own world of restricted vision. We have to be in the world, but not of it, so as to see as God sees. And this means having an eagle eye for the injustices and the traps within the structures of society that marginalise and dehumanise and bind people down. Only by rising above our situation can we speak prophetically to it.

But from the transcendent perspective of over-view we are also to be a people of vision. From a height, imaginatively hovering over the map of the city of Perth and its projected areas of growth between now and the year AD 2001, we can also begin to see and grasp something of the magnitude of what lies before us in the next ten years. And to see the picture whole, with a transcendent view of things, is of course to be struck by the awesomeness of it.

When a new vista opens up before us in the form of the challenge of establishing forty new parishes in the next ten years, we feel something of the awesome impact experienced by John Keates, the romantic poet, when he felt:

> ... like some watcher of the skies
> When a new planet swims into his ken;
> Or like stout Cortez when with eagle eyes
> He star'd at the Pacific – and all his men
> Look'd at each other with a wild surmise –
> Silent, upon a peak in Darien.

To see with eagle eyes from a transcendent perspective naturally fills us with awe; we look at each other silent, upon the peak where God has placed us ... taking in the solemn impact of the possibilities and the responsibilities that lie before us.

To live the transcendent life of Christ is to see more than most, to see prophetically and with heightened vision. But it is also to receive greater challenges than most – to whom much is given much will be required.

Secondly, it was on the eagle's nest on a high and rocky crag that the bird-watchers of the ancient Near East observed the eagle sheltering its young beneath the shadow of its wings, protecting them from the harsh desert heat. They observed the eagle's maternal care of its fragile young and they observed it carrying offspring on its wings from nesting places – high, remote and inaccessible – in order to launch them into life in the real world.

I've seen footage in an ABC television nature program of an eagle-like bird in the Kimberleys, spreading its wings protectively over its young like an umbrella so as to shade its offspring from the searing heat, while its mate hunted for food. This is, of course, an image of sacrifice. The parent bears the discomfort so as to protect and safeguard the young, the fragile and the vulnerable. For the psalmist this eagle image became an image of God's redemption. Over and over the *Psalms* pray for the protection of God's wings, 'hide me under the shadow of your wings' – often the only protective shade available when the heat of human life is on. In Christian confidence we pray a similar prayer for we know that we 'shall be safe under his feathers'.

The image of the eagle ferrying its young from a high and remote place – perhaps secure but arid and without food and sustenance thus making it life-threatening to remain there – in order to bring them into the real world, impressed the author of the book of *Exodus* (19:4):

> After the escape from Egypt, Moses went up to God,
> and the Lord called him from the mountain saying 'this
> you shall say to the house of Jacob and tell the
> Israelites; you have seen what I did to the Egyptians,
> and how I bore you on eagles' wings and brought you
> to myself'.

The bearing of the young on eagles' wings is an image of redemption. God bears us, as on the wings of an eagle, out of slavery into the land of his promise. And we notice that against all false Zionisms of a purely geographical kind, the promised land of God's redemption in *Exodus* is anywhere God himself is, 'I bore you on eagles' wings and brought you to myself.'

When we commence our human journey and are launched into the adventure of life in the land of God's promise, we are delivered from isolation, remoteness, spiritual aridity, anxiety, vulnerability and fear, precisely because God brings us to himself; he ferries us to himself in living community with his people, for God has promised to be wherever his people are.

We are to be prophetic people, seeing with an eagle eye, seeing from the transcendent view point – a people of vision. But we are also to be a redeemed and redeeming people, offering the protective shelter of God, the shade of his wings when the heat is on, and actively ferrying others from remote and humanly arid places so as to launch them into the flight-path of their own life's adventure. As a redeeming people we play our part in bringing others to God himself. We are the eagles of God in all these senses.

Finally, in the ancient world there was a perception that the eagle lived much much longer than any other bird. The extreme length and vigour of its life was explained in an ancient legend that held that the eagle in maturity, at the end of a certain period, moults and by some unknown and mysterious means renews its youth. It is this legendary image that is reflected in *Psalm* 103:5:

> Bless the Lord O my soul …
> Who satisfies your being with good things:
> so that your youth is renewed like an eagle's.

And Isaiah seems to have had the same idea in mind when he said:

> they that wait upon the Lord shall renew their
> strength: they shall mount up with wings as eagles;
> they shall run, and not be weary; and they shall walk
> and not faint.

Raisa Gorbachev in her biography, *I Hope,* says that 'youth is just a moment, but it is also the spark that you always carry with you in your heart'. It is when we become a little daunted, even faint-hearted and aware of our failing energy, that we find ourselves mysteriously renewed. The youthful spark within us is rekindled and we rise up, young and lusty as an eagle.

To set out to establish, in this next decade, forty new parishes in the Diocese of Perth, particularly at this present time of economic recession, rural downturn and general lack of confidence in the Western Australian community; to support, train and ordain forty additional clergy over and above the current levels, and build forty new rectories, and forty new worship centres, and who knows how many new schools and homes for the aged, and on and on ... And to set out to do all this when the demands of humanity upon us are so great, and the need to care for the poor, the unemployed, the alienated and the homeless so pressing, is a daunting task.

Some parishes may even say, 'Oh Archbishop, we are already pushed to keep going ourselves. We are financially strapped; we are faint and weary. We have enough on our own plate without taking on the responsibility of a covenant relationship to assist a new embryonic parish.' Just let us settle down on our perch and ruffle out our feathers, preen them and rest a bit. Or worse, just let us sit on our perch for a while and watch the world go by.

But alas, then we remember the commitment and the enthusiasm of the youthfulness of our faith, and we know that God himself has promised that those who wait upon him and allow their wills to be conformed to his shall renew their strength. They shall mount up with wings as eagles. For youth, although a passing moment, is also a spark that we always carry with us and those who wait upon the Lord shall have their youth renewed like the eagle's.

So from the image of the eagle we discern that we are to be a prophetic people and a people of vision, living the transcendent life of God and *seeing as God sees*.

We are to be a *redeemed and redeeming people*, providing the shelter of God's care, the shadow of his wings and helping to ferry the alienated and vulnerable as on eagle's wings, so as to launch them into their own particular flight-path to the God who ultimately brings us all to himself.

And, in all this we shall know ourselves to be a *renewed people*; for those who wait upon the Lord, in confidence of his promise, like the eagle shall have the strength, energy and enthusiasm of their youthfulness renewed as the chosen recipients of his new life.

That three-fold image of the eagle's prophetic eye, redemptive care and perpetual renewal, and the work to which God calls us in the decade that is before us, I leave with you as we commence this synod. We are truly the West Coast Eagles, the eagles of the divine, a holy people, a royal priesthood, all decked out in the royal blue and gold of God.

9

SNAKES AND SNAILS

PREACHED IN ST GEORGE'S CATHEDRAL, PERTH, ON ALL
SAINTS' DAY, 1 NOVEMBER 1991 AT THE PATRONAL
FESTIVAL OF ST HILDA'S ANGLICAN SCHOOL FOR GIRLS.

I would like to talk to you this morning about snails and snakes.

First snails. I suppose we have all, at one time of our life or another, been intrigued by snails. We have observed their slow progress across a garden path after rain; perhaps we have gently touched their antlers with a twig, so as to watch them spontaneously withdraw into their shell. We have marvelled at the eminent convenience of their ability to carry their mobile homes on their backs, so as to provide both instant protection and accommodation, free of the need that other creatures have to search for it or painstakingly to construct it.

Once, in 1980, I was travelling in France on holiday with my family in the vicinity of Fontainebleau, just south of Paris. We were looking for accommodation for the night and we came to a modest little château, in the forecourt of which some motel-type units had been built. It was out of the tourist season and there was nobody about, and experience had shown that accommodation was hard to find, for at the end of the European winter many hotels and lodging places were either not open or not expecting any guests. However, this looked a nice place as well as interesting, so we tried to knock up the proprietor. Unfortunately, there seemed to be nobody at home despite the fact that all the doors were wide open and the restaurant tables were all more or less set and we felt that somebody was in the vicinity, perhaps even observing us. It was reasonably early in the afternoon and we waited around, and wandered in and out from time to time calling out 'bonjour', 'bonjour madame' … but no answer. The place had that empty eerie feel of a ghost town in a western movie. So we drove away for a few hours and then came back much later in the afternoon in the hope of finding somebody … but still the place was entirely deserted.

We looked into one motel unit through its wide-open door and contemplated moving in to wait there until the owner turned up. It was then that I noticed the silver trail of a snail across the dark brown carpet, the tell-tale sign not just that a lost creature had wandered in from outside and had tracked about the room looking for its escape, but a sure sign that the room had not been used or cleaned for quite some time. The trail of the snail convinced us that perhaps the place was closed until the summer and so we drove on. But the trail of the snail on the carpet remains in my memory of that mysteriously empty and deserted place.

A related sense of unexplained mystery attaches to the large black snail which sits on the mantle in my sitting-room. I bought it one Saturday afternoon from a seller of stones, gems and fossils at a street-side store outside St James' in Piccadilly. It is, as you will guess, an Ammonite from Whitby.

In this particular case it has been cut through in section and polished to reveal the beautiful silver thread of the inner coil and the partitions of the various separate chambers that characterise both this particular kind of ancient sea snail and its long-surviving relative, the Chambered Nautilus. I also have one of these which I picked up a few years ago on the beach at the Cocos Islands.

In the case both of the now extinct Ammonite and the still extant Nautilus, the animal inhabited not the whole shell like a common garden snail but only the first of the series of separate chambers in the shell. And the shell was connected to its back by a long membrane siphon that was threaded through a central hole from chamber to chamber around to the centre of the spiral. If you ever get close to a Nautilus shell you can see the little hole in the wall in the first chamber through which the membrane siphon went. Ammonites were the same. It is really quite fascinating.

Fascination gives way to a sense of awe in the case of the Whitby Ammonite, when one considers its age. The one I bought at Piccadilly is at least 170 million years old … 170 million years. It is certainly the oldest thing in our house.

When one imagines the earth at the time when it was alive, when the sea levels around England were higher than they are now and a large population of Ammonites slowly moved across the rocks in their underwater home, now the shores of Whitby, more than 100 million years before human beings appeared in the evolutionary process, one tends to fall silent. It is difficult to come to terms with the sheer extent of that period of time. As we consider the awesome extent of the evolutionary process we pause in silent wonder.

So snails have always intrigued me. They feature in the memory of a distant and mysterious place; they engender a sense of fascination and awesomeness.

In St Hilda's time the appearance of stone coils in the cliff face along the Whitby shore was no less intriguing, fascinating and mysterious. What were they and how did they get there?

St Hilda, of course, had no knowledge of evolution, not even the remotest hint of it. Only for the last 150 years, since Charles Darwin, have we moderns come to think in terms of evolution. Prior to that, these stone coils, clearly dead animals of some kind but unrepresented among living creatures, had to be explained in other ways.

And so the well known legend arose that they were originally snakes, that St Hilda had decapitated and miraculously turned them in coiled-up form into stone. It was a reasonably good attempt to explain what was otherwise an unexplained and intriguing mystery.

Given that we today account for the Ammonites quite differently as relics of the natural process of evolution, an interesting question is nevertheless thrown up by the ancient legend of St Hilda. Why should St Hilda be so down on snakes? Why should she be moved to turn them all into stone?

Snakes always seem to suffer at the hands of saints. In Ireland there is a legend that St Patrick drove out all the snakes, and this explains what would otherwise be the unexplained mystery of why Ireland, unlike the rest of the world, is entirely snake-free. The amazing thing to me is that St Patrick's spell seems to have so penetrated the Irish soil that it travelled right through the entire globe and out the other side. For New Zealand is also snake-free.

In any event, the fact of the absence of snakes from Ireland is explained and the mystery reduced, if not for us entirely resolved, by recourse to the legend. It is the same in relation to the mysterious appearance of the stone coils we call Ammonites at Whitby.

Behind the legend of St Patrick, as of St Hilda, there is the perception that snakes are bad news; somehow they deserve the fate either of being driven out or turned into stone. Even today we continue to give them a bad press. A certain kind of man is referred to negatively as 'a snake in the grass'; a woman with a vicious tongue is referred to as a 'viper'.

Undoubtedly, the reason for our negative view of snakes is fed by the creation myth in *Genesis* where Adam and Eve are said to have been led astray by a snake. The serpent thereafter became the embodiment of the very devil, the cause of all the world's woes. In the New Testament the devil, Satan, is referred to as 'that old serpent'. No wonder the saints such as Patrick and St Hilda tend to deal severely with snakes.

But if the story of St Hilda turning the snakes into stone is a legend, so too is the story of Adam and Eve and the snake in the *Book of Genesis*. Moreover, our knowledge of the *Book of Genesis* has evolved as a consequence of the work of successive generations of biblical scholars. With their help we now observe that in the actual text of *Genesis* there is no explicit mention that the serpent is to be identified as Satan. That has to be read into it. On the contrary, in *Genesis* the serpent is simply a part of the animal creation, singled out as being more subtle than the other creatures.

Usually, we tend also to think of the indiscretion of Adam and Eve, their disobedience in the Garden of Eden, in moral terms – despite the fact that in the run of things they were created to be husband and wife and were behaving naturally.

In fact, the knowledge of good and evil that the serpent is said to have introduced to Adam and Eve is now known to have been, not moral knowledge, but simply the knowledge of things both good and bad, things beneficial and things harmful to humanity. For the serpent is said to be the most cunning of creatures. He represents not the tempter to moral wrong so much as the stimulus to acquire scientific, technical and factual information. The snake represents the exploring, experimental intelligence, the capacity to be intrigued, to respond to the mystery of the unexplained and to advance hypotheses or theories that are devised to make sense of things. Hence the saying that we must be 'as wise as serpents'. The snake of *Genesis*, as the most cunning of all the creatures, embodies the spirit of scientific enquiry, if you like. The tree of knowledge stands for a knowledge of things. And this is what the serpent caused Adam and Eve to immerse themselves in.

Normally, we regard that as a good thing. It is exactly what education aims at – a knowledge of things, and skills to acquire and increase the knowledge of things. But the story of *Genesis* alerts us to the pitfall of becoming immersed in the pursuit of a knowledge that begins and ends with information about material and creaturely things. For such enquiries stop short of the world of value and the art of managing spiritual interpersonal relationships with wisdom. It has no place for intangibles such as love, care, concern for others.

The problem is that when our minds become immersed in natural science the natural universe tends to be treated as an end in itself, an independent order that can be explained entirely in terms of itself. Of course, very few people are really materialists. You will not find many who will be prepared to contend that matter actually created itself. But many are materialists by default, in the sense that their interests come to rest in material things and go no further.

A knowledge that is content *only* with an understanding of the material surface of the universe, without penetrating to the meaning behind it all, gets involved in the preliminaries but never asks the ultimate question: Why should anything be? Such an attitude of mind inevitably leads to the attempt to live independently of God, as self-sufficient, purely self-interested creatures. That is the attitude of mind that St Hilda is said to have banished by the legendary turning of the snakes into stone.

St Hilda's turning of the snakes into stone reminds us that the exploring, experimental intelligence, which stops short of ultimate questions because of its interest in purely mundane information, important though that can be, has to be kept in its place in a broader context of ultimate mystery and spiritual reality. There is more in heaven and earth than can be discovered by the scientific, exploring, experimental intelligence alone – the meaning of life, the shape of an ultimate human destiny and purpose, the sovereignty of the good above the tawdry, the value of persons, and the need to maintain personal integrity in relationships, the value of love, care and concern for others, particularly those less fortunate than ourself – the whole world of moral value and self-discovery. All this stands behind an interest in purely factual, technical and scientific information. Without it we are turned to stone; we become petrified and dead, superficial souls.

My prayer is that those who graduate from the school communities of our Church will take with them not just information, not just the skills of enquiry and the means to access knowledge – any school could give them that – but an open sense of the broader mystery of life and an orientation to live not just in relation to the material world but in relation to God, and the sovereign values of his will for all of us in the living of our lives.

10

Patterns of Participation: The Trinity and Society

Preached in St George's Cathedral, Perth at the Australian Liturgical Conference Evensong on 5 February 1992.

In my teenage years I worshipped at St James' Church in King Street, Sydney. This was a parish community that was very self-consciously aware of its high standards of worship, particularly the quality of its music, and the near military precision of the movement of ministers and altar servers (of whom I was one) in the sanctuary. In those days we were very well drilled and rehearsed – perhaps over-rehearsed.

Apart from being an altar server I was a member of the very vigorous Young Anglican Fellowship (YAH) which used to meet on Friday night. I cannot recall the details of any one particular Friday night program ... except for one that looms large in my memory.

Father Gabriel Hebert, a monk of the Society of the Sacred Mission, who in the late 1950s taught theology at St Michael's

House, Crafers, in South Australia came to talk to us about lay participation in the liturgy. Even at this point I think I remember his rather eccentric figure – his hooked nose and the white knobbly monkish knees which protruded from under his habit when he hitched it up and dangled his legs over the edge of the table on which he was sitting. Certainly, I remember the way he looked much more clearly than what he had to say.

I do recall, however, that he was very switched on about 'offertory processions'. He clearly believed that the involvement of the laity in the presentation of the gifts of bread and wine was a key focus of their active participation in the liturgy at a very significant moment of the eucharistic action.

During the last week, stimulated by this remnant memory of encounter with Gabriel Hebert in the late 1950s, I took his book *Liturgy and Society* out of the diocesan library to see if what he had to say might give me a point of departure for this sermon. (It is a book that I have not opened for at least twenty-five years.)

To my astonishment I found that it was actually published as early as 1935, and that what Gabriel Hebert had to say on that evening at St James about offertory processions and the involvement of the laity, was already being pushed some twenty years earlier – now nearly sixty years ago.

To my delight, (and perhaps this is more important than lay participation in the offertory), I discovered that the entire book is a forthright attack on theological liberalism, the post-Enlightenment cult of the individual and the general philosophical underpinning of modern liberal democracies in which the individual is given freedom to do his or her own thing, provided he or she does not encroach on any other individual's right to do likewise. Already this contains within it the seeds of the modern notion of the separation of private and public morality, the isolation of the individual from the concept of community, which I happen to think has modern western liberal/democratic society in big trouble – trouble as potentially disastrous in its implications as the current social fragmentation of Eastern Europe.

In any event, this meant that I reread *Liturgy and Society* with a good deal of interest. In it Hebert held up the idea of the liturgy as the instrument for the formation of authentic human community. This was written in the original context of the social fragmentation and confusion and the fall-out of individualism of the mid–1930s in Europe, of which the existentialism of Jean Paul Sartre was one of the more extreme forms. And that is why the book is called *Liturgy and Society*. The Church's liturgy was identified as a social act by which worshippers are brought out of their isolation into fellowship with one another in the Spirit of God. Perhaps that notion has now become so domiciled in our thinking that it does not strike us as particularly new. But what is of particular interest to me is the idea that liturgy, in its role of the formation of the authentic community of the people of God, is seen as a political instrument with a unique power to remake a humane society. And if that need was felt in Europe in 1935, it must surely be felt just about everywhere in the social fragmentation and confusion of today. The gathered worshipping community is the theatre of societal renewal and transformation: in liturgy we remake society.

It is at this point, of course, that the ordination of women to the priesthood comes into focus as an imperative. In the re-made society of the eucharistic community which is inclusive of all without respect to race, colour, gender or class, it is intolerable that women should be repressed and discriminated against.

In any event, it seems to me that were Gabriel Hebert to treat this theme today, his book would contain something that is, in fact, missing from it. *Liturgy and Society* is not just a sociological study without theological landmarks, theological trig stations, as it were, from which we might take our bearings. There is plenty of mention of the worship of God, the mystery of God and the corporate human response to that mystery. But it is remarkable for us today because there is almost no interest in the doctrine of the Trinity. And I want to suggest that if liturgy is an instrument for the re-making of society, surely the fundamental Christian doctrine of God, and particularly our modern interest in the social concept of the Trinity, has something important to say.

When I was approached to say something at this service, it was suggested to me that I might say something about the conference theme of participation or 'something about what needs to be held on to at all costs in an age of liturgical change'. The Trinity gives me the opportunity to say something about both.

The doctrine of the Trinity, it seems to me, is *the* fixed theological datum upon which to keep an eye as we engage in liturgical change, precisely because of its relevance to human *inter*dependence. It is the pattern of participation in community whereby we in liturgy remake society.

Let me say what I mean. It has often been said that there are three ideal types of human community. First there are those communities that secure their common life at the expense of the individual's freedom. A common life is sustained by requiring or imposing a conformity of thought and behaviour. A totalitarian state, or a strictly authoritarian regime, such as we hear of in Iran or see developing in Singapore, would be an example of such a community. The unity of the community is achieved, but at the individual's expense.

Unhappily the Church in some periods of its history has exhibited the characteristics of this kind of community. Even in some parts of the contemporary Church a strict uniformity of view is imposed upon its individual members, to the point where their individuality is absorbed or lost in the life of the whole.

Then at the opposite end of the spectrum, there are those communities that are barely communities at all. Rather, they are very loose associations of individuals, or loose-knit federations of people, who choose to come together in order to achieve some goal or purpose, but otherwise have very little in common. A club, such as a golf club, in which members are locked in bitter rivalry and 'hate one another's guts' but continue to come together for the purpose of playing golf, would be an example of such a community. It would be little more than the aggregate of the individuals who are its members. Some political parties exhibit the characteristics of this kind of community from time to time. I guess the Church has at times also experienced its own community life at such a low temperature as to be little more than a group of individuals who have nothing more in common than the formal pursuit of their individual salvation, which happens to bring them into close proximity from time to time ... say for an hour or so on Sundays.

Then between these two extremes there is that kind of community in which a balance is struck between the interests of the group and the interests of the individual, where individuals are free to be themselves and to think their own thoughts, but in which they freely choose to be together in an ever-deepening set of human relationships. This is a community of individuals who unite, not by any coercive force or just in some trivial pursuit, but by mutual self-gift.

Now, this third ideal type of community is the ideal which the Church seeks to actualise and which I believe we actually glimpse in our concrete experience of life in the eucharistic community, at least from time to time, and especially in its liturgy.

To be a Christian is to be an individual-in-community, a community in which we experience a sense of individual worth. The community life itself is experienced as a zone of freedom in which we have psychological space to be ourselves but in which, as distinct individuals, we freely choose to engage with one another in love and mutual concern, so as to experience that unity of being by self-gift in which we know ourselves to be real persons, and members one of another.

Now, this ideal community is not just something we choose as the ideal most appropriate for the Church. It is not just an ideal we conjure up as we seek in our liturgy to remake society. There is a sense in which it is given to us, and in which its actualisation is laid upon us as a constant and unavoidable obligation. The Church is not just any kind of community or barely a community; it is of necessity a particular kind of community. For the ideal of community which the Church should be, and in which we participate together in human inter-dependence, is given to us precisely in the very central and distinctively Christian doctrine of God – the doctrine of the Holy Trinity.

I suppose when we think of the Trinity we think of the inherited formula – God is three persons and one substance. Just what kind of image that conjures up in your mind's eye is anybody's guess. For me it suggests three distressed people struggling to extricate themselves from a very sticky tub of tapioca pudding. What else can three persons in one substance be?

Perhaps a more helpful way of thinking of God the Holy Trinity was given to us in AD 374 by St Basil of Ceasarea (Basil the Great) in his famous treatise *On the Holy Spirit*. In this treatise Basil spoke, not just of three persons and one substance, but of three persons and one communion – three distinct persons, Father, Son and Holy Spirit, each of whom is not absorbed to the point where all individuality is lost but who are united in one unity of being. The three participate in the one life. The three are one by virtue of the fact that they share a common will and a common purpose; they are one in a common exchange of love. The ensuing communion of mutual self-gift is the essence of divinity. In other words, the idea of personal inter-dependence, inter-personal communion, is a picture of the nature of divinity.

For example, Basil speaks of the Son doing the Father's will, not as a subordinate who has, begrudgingly, to obey a superior out of a sense of duty, but as one whose own will *coincides* with the Father's will. In him the Father finds his own will reflected back to himself like the image in a mirror. So there is no sense of subordination or unwilling compliance or duress, but a perfect reflection by the Son of what the Father wills … and yet the Father and Son are distinct persons. This then is the model of true community as distinct persons united in one communion by self-gift that the Church should reflect in its own life and liturgy. This is the ideal that we hold before our mind's eye as we seek to remake society.

Now there is just one more thing that I want to draw to your attention about the relevance of the doctrine of the Trinity of three persons and one communion for us. It is not just that the Church is meant to *reflect* something of the life of the Trinity in its own life and worship. It is not that the society that is remade in the liturgy reflects the social Trinity. Rather, the Church's inner, spiritual life *is* the divine life of the Trinity. By baptism into Christ we have access to the very life of the Trinity; we are called into it. The gift of the Spirit is the gift to us of divine life in the Church. As people are drawn into the life of the Church, they are actually drawn into a spiritual communion that is the divine life itself. And that happens particularly in the liturgy. At our eucharistic celebration we enter more profoundly into that communion which is divine and that is why we call it precisely the Holy Communion. It is the communion of the Holy, the communion of God in which we participate.

This means that whenever we glimpse true human community in the life of the Church, wherever human individuals are at one, participating together at the deepest possible level, living in harmony and peace of their own free will, by free choice involved in an ever-deepening association with one another in love and concern by mutual self-gift, then we encounter God. In liturgy our participation is precisely in the life of God.

It is not that the Holy Trinity is some remote God whose life as three persons in one communion we yearn to see reflected on earth in the life of the Church; certainly, we do not create it by working at it ourselves. It is rather that God, the Trinity of three persons and one communion, eternally dwells with us and calls us into his very own life, to share it and experience it. Thus we are able to say that the community life of the Church is at its best when it lives closest to its ideal, providing an actual glimpse of the divine life, revealing itself among us.

This is why it is that the pure in heart 'shall see God'. That is why whenever two or three agree on earth it is done in heaven (for heaven and earth coincide), and where two or three are gathered in Christ's name, he is there giving access to the divine life of the Father. But this also means that to deny the importance of the unity of the Church, or to turn one's back on it, walk away from it or cause division in the Church, is really a denial of God himself. Enmity and division is a denial of God. Division is not just a sign of human failure, it is a sign of infidelity, a denial of the reality and presence of God in our midst.

I did not begin with a text so let me finish with one, a Trinitarian one: Our fellowship, our communion, is not just with one another but with God through Jesus Christ our Lord by the gift of the Holy Spirit *(1 John* 1:3, 6–7).

11

THE YELLOW WALLPAPER

PREACHED IN ST GEORGE'S CATHEDRAL, PERTH ON 7 MARCH 1992, ON THE OCCASION OF THE ORDINATION OF AUSTRALIA'S FIRST WOMEN PRIESTS, ALONG WITH ONE MALE CANDIDATE, THE HUSBAND OF ONE OF THE WOMEN.

Charlotte Perkins Gilman was born in 1860. In 1892, at the age of thirty-two, she published a little autobiographical piece entitled *The Yellow Wallpaper*.

It provides me with the first of three images which I wish to hold before you today.

The Yellow Wallpaper is a product of the feminism of that era, exactly a century ago. It is the story of a young woman's mental breakdown, narrated with superb psychological and dramatic precision. Indeed, it is a story to 'freeze your blood' as one commentator said in 1920.

Charlotte Perkins wrenched this small literary masterpiece from her own experience, though many of her other literary works are purely fictional or socio-political. She wrote a book called *Women and Economics*, for example, a witty and bitingly satirical analysis of the situation of women in her society. She was also a very active and apparently inspiring lecturer. As one historian has said, she was perhaps the 'leading intellectual in the women's movement in the United States in her time'.

She was in touch with the suffrage movement, but generally speaking, she found its objectives far too limited. She was much more concerned about the subtle dehumanising pressures imposed by the role assigned to the wife in the conventional and respectable middle-class nineteenth century marriage. She therefore worked independently to expose those dehumanising pressures as well as the incompetent medical advice given by her husband who was a general practitioner, advice which kept her in her place of bondage despite his well meaning intentions. Indeed, the well meaning, benign paternalism of her husband becomes chillingly sinister as one realises that it is actually the cause of his wife's mental breakdown.

He insists, after the birth of a child, when she is grappling with post-natal depression that, 'Bless her heart', she should spend some time in the country. She needs, he tells her, to rest up, do nothing and just get herself together.

She finds herself sleeping in a large country house in an attic room with barred windows, because it had formerly been a nursery, but she lies awake at night feeling trapped by the room's sickly yellow wallpaper. The yellow wallpaper has a mottled design on it which, in her sleepless boredom, she imagines to be all sorts of things, but predominantly, somehow a woman. She sees herself in the wallpaper as the moon shines through the windows and the bars fall in shadows across the yellow wallpaper as in a prison cell.

Secretly she _beings_ to write with clinical precision about the despair experienced as she directly confronts the sexual politics of the male-female, husband-wife relationship at a time when few writers felt free to do so, at least so candidly.

She yearned to be in work, to be mentally stimulated, to engage with people, to be earning a living and making herself useful. What she yearns for is in the language of the Christian Gospel – liberation – and not resting up, confined by role, passively going around the bend.

At the end, she locks the door to her room from the inside and throws the key out through the barred window. And then, as one reads, she goes progressively and disturbingly insane. She moves around and around the walls of the room tearing off the wallpaper with her fingernails, desperately trying to release the woman somehow imprisoned inside by the pattern ... the woman who is herself.

In the end her husband gets the key and opens the door to find all the wallpaper up as far as she could reach entirely stripped off. Her benignly prescribed, submissive, middle-class role has led to her self-destruction.

The implications of the philosophy that women should stay in their place, maintaining silence, concealing problems and repressing creativity, are made perfectly clear in the taut, distraught sentences of her descent into madness. It is an extraordinary piece of writing.

Today, we are peeling away the sickly yellow, faded, silverfish-ridden wallpaper with which the Church has surrounded itself and imprisoned its women for centuries in its benign and perhaps well meaning determination to confine them by role. We are peeling away the wallpaper in order to liberate women from the well-intentioned but humanly diminishing stereotypes in which they have been bound.

Many of those to be ordained today confess that they have entertained a calling to priesthood from an early age, in some cases as early as eight or twelve years, but have suppressed it under the pressure of the belief that women, 'God bless them', cannot possibly be called to such a vocation and ministry. It is a social and ecclesiological impossibility. Today, we are at last declaring, 'It is not!'

Not every woman is called, of course, to a priestly vocation because our God is, as some of the critics of the ordination of women have said, a God of particularity who does not repeat himself in what he does, and calls some but not others. But our experience is that, when measured by the criteria by which we judge the vocation of a man, some women certainly do receive that very same calling.

And those few who are chosen for the ministerial priesthood are a sign and encouragement to other women to exercise their skills and creativity and bring their gifts in various ways to minister to others in love and care. Today, we ordain ten, but we liberate tens of thousands from the stereotypes with which they have been bound so as to free them to move into the glorious liberty of the children of God.

Charlotte Perkins Gilman wrote exactly one hundred years ago this year. My second image is from five hundred years ago.

Last December I spent three weeks at an Inter-Anglican Doctrinal Consultation on, of all things, authority in decision making in the Anglican Communion, a subject about which I have learned a lot in recent days! It was held in the United States at the Virginia Theological Seminary, just across the Potomac River from Washington. At the very same time there was a splendid exhibition at the National Gallery in the Smithsonian Institution in Washington, an exhibition entitled *Circa 1492*.

Among the exhibits was the single surviving copy of Martin Waldseemuller's wood-cut map of the world of 1507. As Europeans struggled to integrate the revolutionary data that reached them in the era post-Columbus, Waldseemuller's map was the first to suggest that Columbus and his contemporaries had, in fact, reached not the western end of the East Indies but a new continent previously unknown to Europe.

Believing incorrectly that the Italian explorer Amerigo Vespucci had preceded Columbus, Waldseemuller named the new continent 'America' after him.

The fact that the earth was a globe had, of course, been known in learned circles throughout the Middle Ages. Only in popular thought do we find the notion that it was flat. The geographers who doubted that Columbus could sail west from Europe to the Indies simply believed the distances to be too great. Columbus surprised himself by reaching the landfall that he thought was his destination in quick time.

As I inspected this priceless map of *Circa 1492*, I observed that Australia was, of course, simply not there at all. The expanding horizons of Europe had yet to embrace the prospect of the Great South Land.

This reminds us that we rarely know what may lie across the horizon of the future. To those who think they know it all, or think that no further developments are possible in the life of the Christian Church, we must simply say in Oliver Cromwell's words, 'By the bowels of Christ we beg you to reconsider; you may be mistaken.' Indeed, we may all yet be surprised at what lies ahead in the future of God – the God of hope who promises to make all things new.

Today, we are all moving towards the new global perspective of an expanding horizon, opening up a new world for the Church.

The Anglican Church, despite its reverence for tradition, is certainly not the kind of Church in which nothing can happen for the first time. And the Church of today positively needs the contribution of women in all aspects of its life. When one thinks about it, given an aging population and a proportionately diminished number of men in the workforce, the need of women to make up the deficit is an absolute imperative in purely statistical terms. Few institutions could survive today without their contribution and input. Think of any bank or school or university minus their women workers – they would probably come to an abrupt halt.

Up until now the Church has been able to struggle on with an exclusively male priesthood systematically depriving itself of half its potential talent. Today our horizon is expanding. Worlds of Christian service and ministry will open up that have not yet been dreamed of.

In the Diocese of Perth we are in growth mode. We are opening a new school every year, our total welfare budget now brushes $20 million annually and we are planning forty new parishes in this current decade. That is 50 per cent more parishes than we now have in the city of Perth. Last year we opened six of the forty. Is it any wonder that the Church began responding about ten years ago to the idea that God was calling women to ministerial priesthood even though at the time we did not really perceive the reason why?

Today will also be a day of expanding horizons in the lives of the ordinands themselves who will enter upon a new ministry involving presiding over the life and worship of a Christian community and no longer just being a deacon assistant to a priest who is always a man. They will enter upon the ministry of pronouncing the forgiveness of God in the ministry of reconciliation and they will bestow his blessing on those who feel alienated and in need of restoration and wholeness. No longer will they as deacons-in-charge of parishes be forced to trek to the nearest male priest to get the consecrated bread and wine of the Blessed Sacrament doing, as in one case, a round trip of some 800 kilometres in the heat and dust each time. That travel time will be much more productively spent.

Today is a day of expanding horizons and new global perspectives. We are naturally conscious that this is a day as historic for us as that day which marked the beginning of the modern world when Columbus sailed west in 1492.

The third image I wish to hold before you is an image of nearly 1800 years ago. On this very day, 7 March in the year AD 203, a group of young women, of whom the identifiable leader was named Perpetua, her companion Felicitas and some others, along with their parish priest, were martyred together in Carthage in North Africa.

These women had felt called by God to become catechumens. They were enrolled to be taught the Christian faith by their priest as preparation for baptism. That was their crime. For it, they gave their lives at the hands of civil authorities in a baptism of blood and fire. Today we still remember them as Perpetua and Her Companions, Martyrs.

The Greek root of the word 'martyr' means 'witness' – one who bears witness in steadfastness of faith to Christ himself and the values of the Christian Gospel. We have come to confine its use to those whose witness was 'unto death'. But the primary meaning is simply to 'bear witness'.

Those whom we ordain to the priesthood today – Elizabeth, Kay, Pamela, Jennifer, Teresa, Catherine, Judith, Joyce, Robin, Elizabeth and Robert, are a group of women and one male, who in witness to the faith of Jesus Christ are laying down their lives. Henceforth they will give their very lives as witness to the unchanging values of the Gospel – love, joy, peace, gentleness, humility in leadership and above all an unwavering commitment to the service of others.

Priestly ordination includes the laying down of other worldly pursuits and preoccupations so as to centre one's life prayerfully on Christ alone, the study of the scriptures, and for the administration of the sacramental tokens of God's presence among us, the end being the worship of God and the good of his people. Ordination rightly occurs in the context of the celebration of the laying down of lives of ancient martyrs.

Putting these three images together we have a triad of liberation, expanding horizons and priestly witness. Today is the day of the glorious liberation of the children of God from the cloying and sickly yellow wallpaper of stereotype with which women have been wrapped around; we peel it off the walls!

Today is the day of expanding horizons and of new global perspectives, for the candidates themselves, for women generally, for the Church in this Diocese of Perth and in Australia and for the world of the future.

And today is a day of witness, the laying down of lives for the service of others, an image and token in the present of the eternal self-giving of Christ himself, the great high priest who ever lives to plead his sacrifice for us, the one for the many, who lays down his life for his friends, which is the essence of priestly service.

May God richly bless Elizabeth, Kay, Pamela, Jennifer, Teresa, Catherine, Judith, Joyce, Robin, Elizabeth and Robert, and all we today do together to the glory of his great name.

12

ON BEING SPIRITUALLY AMBULANT

PREACHED AT ST GEORGE'S CATHEDRAL, PERTH ON SUNDAY 21 JUNE 1992, TO CELEBRATE THE CENTENARY OF THE ST JOHN AMBULANCE SERVICE IN WESTERN AUSTRALIA (1892–1992).

The celebration of one hundred years of history of the St John organisation in Western Australia puts us in touch with a broad tradition of care that goes back to a time well before the present day.

The word 'ambulance' is a nineteenth century word that was not often used before the Crimean War. It came to be used of the wagons or carts that conveyed the injured from the field of battle. Some heroic examples of the transportation of the sick to a place of care on the back of an animal have also become part of our story. I think, for example, of Simpson and his donkey.

But behind that historical image of the field ambulance in time of war, stands the timeless prototype of all ambulance services in societies of Christian origin; the paradigm of the

Good Samaritan who administered first-aid, provided the ambulance service and, by undertaking to pay the bills himself, even headed off the inevitable question on the innkeeper's lips, 'Are you with HBF?'

Ambulances take people to where they need to be in order to access continuing care; by definition they move people from A to B. And, insofar as the St John organisation majors in first-aid, it implies a second level of care somewhere else.

Within the ideals of the St John organisation, and implicit in the very concept of an ambulance service, there is thus a dynamic of movement – from the field of battle to aid-post, from curbside to hospital, from first-aid to the next aid … from injury to health.

I draw your attention to this dynamic of movement for a purpose. There was a time when the whole of human life was understood in terms of movement. We were encouraged to see ourselves-as-we-happened-to-be and ourselves-as-we-could-be-if-we-reached-our-God-intended-purpose as two quite different things. Or, if we were not theists, we saw ourselves-as-we-happened-to-be and ourselves-as-we-could-be if we simply reached our higher human potential as two quite different things. Human life itself was seen as a journey; it was understood in terms of moving morally and spiritually from A to B, as it were.

And in order to assist us on our way, the clarification and teaching of moral values was an integral and important part of our education. We were brought up to aspire to virtue and to avoid vice. That was how we made the transition from where-we-happen-to-be to what-we-might-become.

Indeed, whether we are conscious of it or not, we are heirs to a moral tradition in which seven fundamental virtues were valued in particular. There were the four cardinal virtues – prudence, temperance, justice and fortitude – that could be grasped unaided by human reason, topped up, for those open to the gift of grace, by the three theological virtues – faith, hope and love.

As it turns out, the four cardinal virtues that were traditionally held up before every reasonable man and woman as values worth striving for as he or she moved towards the perfective destination of life's journey, are precisely the four virtues that are symbolised in the organisation's iconography in the four arms of the Cross of St John. Prudence, because an ambulance person needs the reflective ability to make considered, cool-headed judgments; temperance, because he or she needs to be able to temper his or her feelings so as not to be hassled by emotion, with a mind unconfused by the immediacies of passion; justice, because he or she must be prejudice-free and prepared to deliver care without fear or favour to any needy human person; and fortitude, because all this must ideally be done with sustained dedication to task – or steadfast strength of purpose.

The four cardinal virtues thus have particular significance as ideals to which ambulance men and women have traditionally been exhorted to aspire; but the same virtues, of course, have a more general application to all of us.

Now, my suspicion is that talk of the four cardinal virtues, or indeed talk of aspiring to human virtue generally, will fall to your ears as something quaintly strange, even just a little antique – almost as quaintly strange as the antique cloaks in which members of the Order are prone to parade on occasions such as this.

And that gets me to the nub of what I really want to say this morning.

Talk of the human virtues, whether cardinal or theological, or of virtues over and above the traditional seven, strikes us all as just a little passé. It is not the kind of talk we have heard much of lately. This is because there is a real sense in which contemporary liberal/democratic western societies have all moved, in a socially significant sense, away from a morality of virtue.

Moreover, we do not identify, dwell upon and uphold the virtues, whether in our adult communications with one another or in teaching morality to the young, precisely because we no longer think in terms of moving from A to B, from where humans happen to be to where they might aspire to be in order to actualise their God-intended or higher purpose. In our self-understanding we are no longer spiritually and morally ambulant.

It is because generally speaking we no longer think of human life in terms of an ambulative, perfective schema of moral and spiritual movement that the teaching of the virtues no longer features in the curriculum of our schools. By and large an education in the clarification of values disappeared overnight in post-World War II Australia; by the late 1960s it was fast becoming a thing of the past in secondary education and in many, if not most, of this nation's primary schools as well. A moral education simply dissolved away, along with the religious instruction in schools with which it was inextricably bound, for the virtues are normally taught through the stories of a religious tradition. The parable of the Good Samaritan is but one of them.

The result is that in society at large these days we no longer teach or even talk about the virtues because the framework of spiritual and moral movement which provided them with their appropriate context and rationale, has long since been abandoned.

You may ask, 'With what has it been replaced?'

Well, instead of the schema of ambulant progress from

A to B, from where one happens to be to where one might be if one were to approximate more closely to one's higher or God-intended purpose, we tend more characteristically today simply to focus on where we happen to be.

It has been said that whether you are Catholic, Protestant, Jewish or entirely secular in outlook, it makes very little real difference. Religion has become a superficial overlay, for deep down we have all become small 'l' liberals; we are all children of the Enlightenment. As Alastair MacIntyre has said, some of us are conservative liberals, others liberal liberals, others radical liberals, but all are deep down small 'l' liberals. For, the most characteristic form of moral discussion in western liberal democracies takes the form, not of a consideration of virtues, but of a discussion of 'rights'.

Since the Enlightenment and particularly over the last one hundred years we have become accustomed to upholding and defending human rights of all kinds that are thought somehow to inhere in the natural person, the individual where he or she happens to be. Our current concept of what it is to be a human being is thus very static.

We have become familiar with successive statements of rights in liberal/democratic societies: civil rights, women's rights, land rights, the right to an education, the right to work, the right to choose one's own lifestyle, the right to adequate health care. The moral officers and guardians of such a society are human rights commissioners, and we put considerable energy into drawing up bills and charters of rights such as the United Nations Charter on the Rights of the Child. I even heard a chap on the radio say that he was attempting to draw up a bill of rights for taxpayers!

Now there may well be a place for some form of talk of rights. But I happen to think that the eclipse of virtue and our contemporary near-exclusive concentration on an ethic of natural rights may, in fact, be quite disastrous.

For a start, to focus simply on rights and to forsake any interest in the virtues becomes excessively and very dangerously individualistic. The rights that are to be preserved are always the rights of individuals. Indeed, our overriding concern since the Enlightenment has been to protect the individual against interferences and encroachments on individual freedoms by society at large. The individual and his or her good inevitably, therefore, tends to be valued above what may be thought good for society as a whole. The result is that in discussions of rights society tends to be presented negatively, almost always as a threat to the individual, whose rights must be defended at all costs.

In the world of economics this leads to modern economic rationalism and the current obsession with a free market economy, for the individual has the right to be free of community interference so as to allow uninhibited growth in economic matters. Whether that individual right can be sustained in the face of the growing community concern about the world environment, only time will tell.

It is in the area of morals, however, where societies committed to liberal individualism are most clearly on the precipice of the disaster of breaking up from within. In such societies the individual must be free to espouse a private morality provided he or she does not encroach on another person's equal rights and freedoms, and all of us must be prepared to be tolerant of more diversity. Inevitably, this individualism leads to contemporary moral pluralism.

My problem with this is that from a societal point of view it may hold within itself the seeds of society's own destruction. So long as we are simply exhorted to tolerate a wide range of moral alternatives, moral debate is subtly stifled. It has been said that a liberal is a man who leaves the room when an argument begins; he is too broad-minded even to take his own side in a quarrel. Indeed, the passively tolerant acceptance of alternatives of moral pluralism effectively means that the concept of moral truth goes out the window.

In other words, a discussion of what exactly is virtue, what precisely is just, what is temperate and what is steadfast in particular kinds of situations, and why these things might be valued in a community and upheld as community values and commended to the young in schools or in spiritual direction, slips away in all our talk of an individual's 'rights'. This has become our staple moral diet – the preoccupying subject of endless conferences and discussions.

The resultant contraction of moral debate and the excessive individualism of moral pluralism is thus one side of the penny. The other side is the diminishment of a sense of moral community and the near abandonment of any attempt to hammer out shared community standards of right and wrong, good and bad, on the anvil of rational enquiry. Instead we hear the ever more strident rhetoric of the assertion of competing view points.

When tolerance breaks down, the competing groups of a pluralistic society simply become more shrill and assertive. That is why at one end of the spectrum protest has become the characteristic form of expressing political dissent in western liberal democracies and at the other end of the spectrum, instead of the rational weighing of argument, politics have become a matter of trying to demonstrate the personal ineptitude of one's opponents.

Given our acquiescent acceptance of moral pluralism we should not be surprised that we have become very reticent about upholding community standards and tardy about teaching any morality to the young. Self-fulfilment – freedom to do one's own thing – has become more a matter of allowing the individual to decide his or her own lifestyle. And should we not simply tolerate individual freedoms and all alternative private moralities? For who are you to tell me how I am to live?

Today I want to put in a plea for a more communitarian approach to morality, in which what is good for individuals is not automatically juxtaposed to what may be good for society at large. Rather, they may be worked out together, within a unitary vision of the good. Before we jump into the discussion of the alleged 'rights' of individuals, we have to have an eye to the kind of community we desire to produce.

For there are signs that all is not well in the liberal democracies of the western world. Given the collapse of communism in Eastern Europe, we may well feel that things are fine on our side of the East/West divide. But that is an illusion. I fear one only has to think of rising crime and anxiety about increasing levels of violence and social fragmentation, the apparent impotence of mechanisms of juvenile justice to maintain order, the pollution of the environment, the levels of stress to which people are subject, the persistent spread of drugs, the scourge of AIDS, increasing divorce and the tragic fragmentation of families on a scale unprecedented in human history, and the apparent contemporary human inability to sustain relationships, to see that the modern liberal/democratic societies of the West are in big trouble. Indeed, something like the break-up from within of the Roman Empire when civilisation survived only by the skin of its teeth may well be looking at us down the barrel of the future.

The fact that riots in Los Angeles could have happened in any one of a dozen similar centres in the United States and that in that country, the mother of all liberal democracies, there are now thirty-seven million people living below the poverty line, is sufficient alone to suggest that all may not be well with liberal individualism.

In the world of liberal individualism a consideration of a life of virtue not only becomes wholly passé, but more difficult even for individuals to attain in practice. It is more difficult to love one's neighbour when the trend of the whole cultural context is to assert one's right to exploit one's marketplace advantage and to see one's neighbour simply as one's economic rival.

However, wherever an ambulance vehicle or station displays the badge of St John, with its cross, signalling the fundamental virtues of prudence, temperance, justice and fortitude, a statement is being made. We rightly celebrate one hundred years of the culture and ideals of the St John organisation.

For these are the virtues to which those in ambulance stations across the nation aspire. Those people who, like the Good Samaritan, are dedicated to love of neighbour. Towards the attainment of that set of virtues we may all profitably seek to move as we grasp again the possibilities of an ambulative, perfective humanity and work together to build a morally alert and compassionate community.

It is precisely in the languishing world of liberal individualism, mugged by a morality of 'rights' alone in which humanity is rendered immobile and static, that the virtues come to our aid to be valued and cherished and celebrated and upheld, to direct and perfect our behaviour.

And this, of course, is exactly why we are here today – to trumpet a tradition of one hundred years and to look ahead to taking that moral tradition with us in the years that are to come.

13

THE COLOUR GREEN

PREACHED AT THE OPENING EUCHARIST OF THE SECOND
SESSION OF THE FORTY-FIRST SYNOD OF THE DIOCESE
OF PERTH, 16 OCTOBER 1992.

The colour green is the colour of money. Prior to the introduction of decimal currency into Australia in the 1960s the old one pound note was green, as was its sterling equivalent. Visitors to North America find United States dollars a little difficult to differentiate by denomination precisely because all bank notes are engraved in black on white; but the undersides of American dollar bills also retain the traditional colour of green – hence the 'American greenback'. So the colour green is the colour of money.

The colour green, however, is also the colour of ecology. It denotes unhindered growth, free of all pollution and inhibiting factors introduced by human occupation of this planet. Hence all those around the world who fly the colour green in the cause of the protection of the environment.

And there is a certain tension between the banknote green of the economy and the growth green of ecology. Until very recent years to be 'green' was automatically to be classified with a minority of troublesome enthusiasts who were thought to be anti-capitalist, anti-free enterprise, against logging in rain forests, against mining interests, and generally against the making of money and the growth of the economy. A fundamental human concern and anxiety has, however, now gripped us and changed things. The celebrated hole in the ozone layer, the release into the atmosphere of harmful gases by the burning of fossil fuels and the consequent tendency of the earth to overheat, the ensuing risk of cancer, the observable contraction of glaciers in the Italian Alps, and the possible melting of the southern ice cap and the prospect of the flooding of coastal cities has radically changed our attitude. Suddenly 'greenies' have become respectable. Indeed, in a sense we have all taken on something of the ecological hue of the colour green.

And I suppose that all this is only natural; for humankind like other species of animal, is motivated by a fundamental instinct of self-preservation. We are all by nature concerned for the future welfare of our children and our children's children on this planet. And so all-embracing is our ecological concern that it overrides the more peripheral issues that differentiate political parties and ideological systems as they jostle to manage the world's economy. Somehow the economic green of the colour of money is beginning to take second place to the ecological green of a future verdant pasture with fresh air, wholesome space in which to survive at all.

What does Christianity have to say about this? As a fearful world grapples with the possibility of self-destruction by its own wilful stretching of the limits of the earth's resources to the point of ecological catastrophe, is there any good news for us to proclaim? I suppose there is always a danger for Church people to say too much too late. In this case it is easy for us to get on the environmental bandwagon and to engage in a good deal of unhelpful hand-wringing and moralising that simply echoes prevailing green concerns. In the Church we are always prone to assimilate our thinking to what is culturally fashionable and simply reflect what is going on in the world around us.

However, historical development can alert us to truths of our own tradition that have hitherto lain dormant. For a start, the green movement can point us to a new sense of our creatureliness. The earth is finite, fragile and relatively small. It is clearly a mistake to imagine that its history will continue for ever. For, as the environmentalist reminds us, the whole created order of which we ourselves are part, exists within certain limits.

Sometimes we imagine, especially when we are young, that our lives will go on forever; and perhaps we have assumed that our world has a limitless future before it as well. But the modern concern about the environment is rooted in the human experience of finitude. We exist for a limited period of time, and the rest of the created order likewise faces the ultimate prospect of a natural end too.

According to the prevailing view of most scientists our universe came to be in a massive explosion and it is still expanding. In a sense it appears limitless, infinite, immense beyond our comprehension. But our planet, as one of the thousands of millions of tiny specks of matter in the vastness of space, faces the prospect of a natural death when the sun's energy eventually peters out and it becomes a 'red giant'.

In other words, God has put finite limits to the endurance of all natural systems, just as he has appointed a limited span of years for each of us to live upon this earth; on average three score years and ten. The prospect of death is something we share with the whole created order. As part of nature we participate in nature's limitation.

Modern environmentalism also reminds us that we ourselves are transient beings. We have no continuing city, we are strangers and pilgrims, sojourners on earth, who do not ultimately belong here. We cannot settle down in this world in a domesticated kind of way, as though it were our ultimate home. We are destined to find our fulfilment in another place, separate from this one. We have responsibilities towards those whom we leave behind.

In a way, our placement in this world, wherever we are, has always been a little like the artificial life of exotic plants in a greenhouse. Like the weeping fig trees in the Trump Tower in New York they have been taken out of the natural environment where they really belong to be cooped up under glass in an alien place.

I wonder if you know the melancholy words of the poem that Richard Wagner set to music as the third of his Wesendonk songs:

> High-arched leafy crowns,
> canopies of emerald,
> Children of a distant clime,
> tell me, why do you mourn?
> Noiselessly your branches bend,
> shaping gestures in the air,
> and as silent witness of sorrow
> there rises upwards a sweet scent.
> Wide in yearning desire
> you spread out your arms
> and embrace the maddening

void horror of empty space.
Well do I know, poor plants,
that we share one destiny,
even with light and glass above us
our homeland is not here!

We are set in this created world like imported plants in a greenhouse. We do not ultimately belong; we are aliens in a foreign place – 'our homeland is not here!' 'You have made us for yourself, O God, and our hearts are restless until they rest in you.'

So much then for what reflection upon the green phenomenon can bring to mind out of our own Christian tradition about our finitude, the limited nature of creaturely existence, and the transience of all things including our own mortal life in this place.

But what can Christians bring to the environmental problems that currently concern us? If the problem of the environment triggers our awareness of our own human predicament of limitation and fallenness, what is our Christian good news?

Perhaps there are some pietistic Christians for whom a concern for the environment is irrelevant. They are content to turn Jesus into a mechanism for getting themselves and a few other human beings to eternal life with God, while the rest are literally left to go to the devil. That, however, is to develop the Christian doctrine of salvation in independence of a doctrine of creation.

If we take off the glasses of 'individual justification' with which, since Luther, we have tended to read the New Testament, we will see that Paul always speaks, not of our individual sins and need for salvation from them, but of sin as an all-pervading gone-wrongness of the whole universe. Just as we share in its finitude we share in its sin, its imperfection. The whole creation groans in travail, and the coming of Christ and his resurrection has to do with its renewal and fulfilment. Its redemption from its fallen imperfect state goes hand-in-hand with the renewal of humanity. The whole creation awaits the revealing of the children of God.

If we share in the limitation and finitude and imperfection of the created order, it in turn benefits from our human renewal in Christ, 'the firstborn of all creation'. Indeed, in the ancient Church the day of Christ's resurrection was sometimes referred to as the eighth day, the day of the restoration of all creation.

To be a Christian disciple is not just to leave this world, though ultimately we must do that, but also to live in faithful obedience to God and his will within it. As the former Bishop of Birmingham Hugh Montefiore has said, 'Disciples of the cosmic Christ cannot become cosmic drop-outs.'

After all, any authentic form of Christian commitment must involve some fundamental belief in creation. Sunday by Sunday we affirm that we believe in God the Father Almighty, maker of heaven and earth. We also inherit a tradition in which we believe that human beings have a unique place in the created order. Did not God place us here to inhabit the earth and subdue it, to exercise a certain dominion over it? Some have tended to assume that 'dominion' means not just to subdue and control unruly nature but to exploit it and plunder it, but our task is actually to tend, manage and care for it as responsible stewards of God.

When our time comes to leave this world we shall all be judged. And whether we believe that judgment to be by God or merely by history, the truth will be the same. And in that reckoning it will not just be the truth about what we have individually become, but what we have made of ourselves corporately and of our world – what stewardship and care of creation we have exercised in the face of our human capacity for selfish exploitation.

We now appreciate that human beings have it within their capacity to destroy the earth and bring it to an unnatural end much more quickly than we dreamed possible even a decade ago. But the end of things is appointed to happen in God's good time; in the fullness of time according to his purpose. A violent and premature end, produced by human sinfulness and mismanagement, is as frustrating to the divine plan as the premature, unnatural or violent death of a human being.

Our fundamental Christian belief in creation and the goodness of the natural order therefore involves us in an acknowledgement of our responsibility as the managers and stewards of it.

Of course, the need for stewardship is now obvious and urgent. The days of unchecked exploitation of our natural resources are over. This means that we cannot accept a philosophy of unlimited economic growth as the fundamental motivation of the political order. Politicians and advertisers have no right to put this goal before us. Unrestricted free enterprise uninhibited by public constraint has no brighter future than the neglectful incompetence of Eastern Europe.

As Hugh Montefiore, says:

> All too often the appeal of politicians and that of
> advertisers in the mass media, is to greed and
> acquisitiveness. This seems to breed envy and
> covetousness and therefore to lead to frustration and
> unhappiness, which in turn increases pressure for more

economic growth as a mistaken means of putting things right. We can get caught up in a vicious spiral of mistaken aspirations and unintended results.

The tension between ecological crisis and economic growth will only be resolved by the reorientation of humanity away from a desire to amass more and more things, and towards a determination to become more and more human.

A reorientation of this kind is, of course, what we Christians mean by repentance: it is a fundamental turning, a conscious rejection of all that is life-denying and thus evil in favour of an alignment with what we discern to be God's sovereign will for us and the good of all humankind. And in the world of consumerism repentance of this kind entails the five 'r's: recycle, reuse, repair, replant and rejuvenate.

Thus we Christians do have a message for a world concerned and anxious about the environment. And we cannot be accused of saying too much too late; rather we say relatively little and what we say is what we have ever said, 'Repent, for the kingdom of God is at hand.' The way of redemption both for us humans and for the natural order is a call to repentance, a reorientation of attitude on a planetary scale to turn away from all that is selfish and life-denying. It involves a preparedness for some self-sacrifice. But is also an announcement of good news. For it is a call to turn towards the kingdom of God which we joyously announce to be at hand.

In other words, our call to men and women of all nations to turn towards the dawning kingdom of God, to align themselves with the sovereign will of God and to dwell together in unity, is fundamental to solving the world's current ecological problems. This is why Paul says that the whole creation awaits with eager anticipation the revelation of the children of God. For the simple truth is that there can only be a wholesome future for the earth if people of all nations act together to preserve the environment. It is no good having legislation against pressure packs with CFCs here in Australia if they are going to continue in use elsewhere. However, men and women can act together only if they are first committed to living together in love and peace.

In order to solve the ecological crisis we must first therefore see men and women of all the nations of the earth as our companions. The word companion comes from the Latin *com* meaning *with* and *panis* meaning *bread*. Our companions are those with whom we break bread. Human unity of the kind we experience in the Church when we break and share bread together is for us the sign in the present of the coming kingdom of God. In the Church the kingdom is 'at hand', because the Church is itself that part of the world where the sovereign reign of God is already acknowledged and people are thus drawn together in him.

The Christian religion therefore brings to current world concern and anxiety about the environment some good news, not just about the future possibility of human unity that is a prerequisite for solving the ecological crisis, but also about the actual proximity of human renewal and unity of purpose in the kingdom of God. It is in the Church itself that we experience that as a reality that is already coming to be.

Perhaps it helps to make this point, to note that the word ecology and the word economy, despite our tendency to assume a fundamental tension between them, both derive from the same Greek word. It is the word *oikos* meaning house. Those charged with management of the economy are the stewards, those who run the household. Those who share a concern for ecology are concerned that the environment should continue to provide us with a home during our sojourn on earth, an eco-system (*oikos*-system) in which there is a certain harmony and balance – as in any good home.

But there is another significant word of our contemporary vocabulary that also derives from *oikos* (house). It is the word ecumenical – pertaining to the whole inhabited world. For the world to be the place where all human beings can make their home, it must be the place where men and women have the will to live together in unity and peace and the grace to achieve it.

Our hope for salvation from cosmic self-destruction is therefore no abstract bit of wishful thinking because its possibility is already present in an anticipated way in the life of the people of God. The Church as a renewed humanity, living in unity of heart and mind under God, is itself good news, advance publicity of the coming attraction of the renewal of all creation in Christ. That is why the whole creation awaits the revealing of the children of God at the hands of the God of promise who says, 'Behold, I create a new heaven and a new earth.'

It is at this point that there is a connection between ecology, economy, ecumenism and *evangelism*. Our mission as the renewed Israel of God is to bring light and hope to the nations. Unless men and women of *all* the nations of the earth can live together, in accordance with God's sovereign will, there can be no avoiding ecological catastrophe and we shall all perish.

The renewal of humanity, as we glimpse it as the children of the resurrection in love and forgiveness, in unity of heart and mind, in the inclusive life of the catholic Church, is light and hope. The way towards ending structural injustice, towards the sharing of the world's resources, the careful management of the economy, and the nurture of a global determination is to turn from all that is life-denying towards an alignment with human life, renewed and wholesome, and the restoration of all creation, under the perfect reign of God.

The future of the earth and the human redemption we proclaim in our resurrection faith, the renewal of humanity in justice, love and peace, go hand-in-hand. The Church is the anticipation of this, and apart from the Church, understood in this way there is, quite simply, no salvation.

14

LIFE AFTER DEATH

PREACHED AT THE DIOCESAN CONVENTION OF THE DIOCESE OF
ARKANSAS AT LITTLE ROCK, ARKANSAS, ON 20 FEBRUARY 1993.

This morning we are assembled to remember those
members of the family of this Diocese who have died
during the last year. I therefore want you to think about
Christian belief in eternal life.

We affirm this belief each time we say the Creed – when we
say, 'I look for the resurrection of the dead and the life of the
world to come' or 'I believe in the resurrection of the Body
and the life of the world to come.' But I think we have to
admit that these days people tend to take these beliefs a little
lightly.

According to Gallup polls taken in Australia over the last
twenty years, of those who believe in God (currently abut 78
per cent of the Australian population) fewer than 50 per cent
claim to believe in their own personal survival beyond the
grave. I suspect the percentages would be very similar in the
United States.

One reason for this is that many Christians these days prefer to identify with the transforming activity of God for good in this world. They understand their Christian commitment in terms of working cooperatively with God for justice and peace. They think of God's salvation in terms of putting an end to hunger and poverty rather than pursuing God's promise of a better deal in some after-life and leaving the human suffering of this world as it is. Rather than pray, 'Lord take me at the last into your eternal kingdom', they prefer to affirm the Lord's own prayer, 'Your kingdom come, your will be done, *on earth,* as it is in heaven'. They thus focus on this world and the coming of God's transforming reign of justice and peace within it. This means that even for many Christians, God's saving activity in this world is of more concern than salvation in the form of individual survival beyond the grave and the life of the world to come.

For a number of reasons many people these days find it much more difficult to believe in an after-life. It has even been said that men particularly are not so concerned about another life; they are more prone to yearn for another wife!

Certainly, the concerns of historical life in this world and the art of managing relationships are all-absorbing and all-consuming. We are less and less inclined to stop and reflect about the significance for us of death as the absolute termination of the interpersonal hassles of our historical existence.

Moreover, perhaps as a result of modern medicine, we tend to live with the illusion that life will go on, if not for ever, then for a very extended future. In Jesus' day the unknown world beyond the Mediterranean seemed so fearsome; and without the advances of modern medicine, life within it was so much more precarious than our life today. When people are accustomed to the death of their contemporaries at almost every stage of their life, and the average life expectancy is less than twenty-five, *then* death is much more a normal part of life. As Thomas Hobbes said, the life of man is 'nasty, brutish and short'. The unavoidable nearness of death forced people to consider it seriously and contemplate what might lie beyond it.

Today, we live longer and more comfortably. We can, to a degree quite unknown in the ancient world, keep death at bay. We can delay the end by heart transplants and kidney transplants and tablets to control our blood pressure. We can extend our historical existence and thus postpone having to face death. Our average life expectancy has been rising – twenty years in the Roman world, thirty-three in the Middle Ages, approximately fifty 100 years ago, and now about seventy-nine or eighty years on average. (It's a little more for women than men.) The trauma of having our contemporaries die around us is less of a reality as we live our lives; it happens more often at the end when we ourselves are old. And even when we do have to deal with death, we tend in the modern world to deflect its impact upon us and our humanity. How many jokes have you heard about death or St Peter at the pearly gates? This is just one way to avoid taking death too seriously.

Some of us spend a good deal of time making death appear less fearsome and threatening, less ultimate. We have developed a modern psychology of death and dying, and instead of dwelling on its significance as the absolute end of our historical existence we tend to focus on the process of dying and ways of making it less traumatic, pain-free, more amenable, even acceptable. Hence the contemporary debate about euthanasia and assisted suicide; the process of dying excites more interest than a debate about what lies *beyond* death.

We also spend a good deal of our time reflecting on ways of ministering to those who remain after the death of a loved one. It is not the after-life, or life after death, but coping with grief after death that is our more characteristic twentieth century preoccupation.

We even keep death at bay by hiring an undertaker to take care of the arrangements, prepare a body for burial and generally soften the impact of the trauma of death upon us: out of sight; out of mind. But undertakers are very modern inventions; formerly the human acquaintance with death was so much more immediate and direct because the detailed funeral arrangements and preparation were in the hands of the mourners themselves.

So in all kinds of ways we tend these days to deal with death at one stage removed. It does not have the impact upon us that it once had. Even when we read of accidents in the press the impact is short-lived – we imagine that it will never happen to us. And if we do not think about the immediacy and apparent finality of death and what it ultimately means for us, then there is less and less likelihood that we will think seriously about life after death.

As a consequence, these days people tend to disengage from the credal affirmation of belief in the resurrection of the body and the life of the world to come. And yet there it is at the end of the Creed we Christians say each time we come to church, 'We look for the resurrection of the dead and the life of the world to come.'

We are, of course, also reminded of this at every eucharist when as heaven and earth come together we join, not just with angels and archangels but the 'the whole company of heaven', the saints of God and all Christian souls, in the one communion of God of the living and the departed. We thus have at least some kind of opportunity to correct our usual attempts, perhaps unconscious, at death avoidance.

So why should we continue, as modern people, to look for the resurrection of the dead and the life of the world to come? Am I going to live or shall I at death vanish like a bubble?

I think people have difficulty in affirming a confident belief in the after-life, not just because they tend to avoid taking death seriously and therefore the possibility of life after death, but because they do not take God quite seriously enough.

It is not easy to believe in the gift of new life beyond the grave if you do not first have a lively faith in an eternal God of love and care. But if God created us and if, as now seems undeniable, we are each unique so that there is no other person who shares our genetic make-up, no other person who is anything like a replica of the unique human self which is each one of us, and if life in this world is not just a chance conglomeration of random happenings but rather an inter-connected unity of purpose, then in the good purpose of the God who created us, we can contemplate the consummation of our personal growth and spiritual development by fulfilment in him.

A great deal hangs upon our uniqueness as individual beings. When you think about it, what is of most value to us, what we believe should be kept and safely guarded in a museum, is the sole existing item – a very rare Chinese vase for example. The mass produced plastic cup is of very little value, but the unique object is worth preserving. And if we are as persons, unique creations of God, then we are, in the eyes of our creator, of infinite value and worth – we are worth preserving! History may write us off, but God does not.

If the transcendent mystery, the unapproachable light, at the heart of the universe has the colour of love, and if we as unique creations of God are of supreme value and worth, then we can begin to contemplate with some confidence the belief that God has prepared a place and a future for us in the life to come.

Moreover, in our Christian understanding, our God is not just loving, and concerned and caring, but trustworthy and reliable. He is not a creature of whim, a God of fits and starts, but a God of steady purpose and steadfast love upon whom we can rely for the consummation of our lives, the completion of the spiritual course of our perfecting, which is only ever partial in our historical lives in this world.

This means that the question of resurrection beyond the grave and eternal life is first of all the question of God and his identity. It is God 'who alone has immortality' (*1 Timothy* 6:16). Any possibility of human immortality depends on him who 'gives life to the world' (*John* 6:33).

Those who, like the Sadducees, went to Jesus with questions about their personal survival beyond death, must therefore first ask questions about the nature of their belief in God. After all, none of us can entrust ourselves to God to give us the gift of eternal life, unless we can first entrust ourselves to him in the immediacy of tomorrow. We cannot entrust ourselves to God in the hereafter, if we do not ground our lives in him here on earth in the immediate future of tomorrow, or even later today.

The first reason why we can still affirm our belief in the resurrection of the body and the life of the world to come, is that we are convinced of the utter trustworthiness of a God whose nature is love and who out of love chose to create us. To create us as unique individuals who in his good purpose are destined to achieve the consummation and completion of our humanity – the perfecting of our humanity in him.

The second reason for our belief in a transcendent life hereafter also has to do with the question of God and his identity. We Christians believe that God is a God of justice. Yet it is a fact that history is full of all kinds of injustices. In their historical existence some people are advantaged, others are disadvantaged. Some have the Gospel preached to them, others do not. Some suffer and hunger and thirst for righteousness; some quite simply hunger and thirst – and God's sovereign and overarching justice must include the putting to right of all injustices.

If God is a God of justice; if, in the context of the universe, justice is an ultimate value, then in the consummation of God's good purposes there must be opportunity for wrongs to be put right, perhaps even opportunities for those who have found it difficult to believe to turn to the saving presence of God and enjoy the blissful rewards of heavenly life.

Once again, the question of the after-life comes down to the question of the identity and trustworthiness of God. The after-life is the unmerited, free consequence of God's utter trustworthiness, whose good purpose can be summed up in the term 'justification' – putting things to right.

And finally, of course, we believe in the resurrection of the body and the life of the world to come because Jesus' resurrection is the promise of our own; we are the 'children of the resurrection'. We know in our corporate life together the impact of Jesus' personality upon us. Just as he called a group of followers about himself in the days before his crucifixion, so we continue to experience his call to gather together around his living presence as the Spirit of our common life and worship. We live because he lives among us and in us. 'I yet not I; Christ in me' (*Galations* 2:20).

And that is why John can say that he who believes in the Son already has life. 'The person who hears my word and believes him who sent me, has eternal life; he does not come into Judgment, but has already passed from death to life' (*John* 5:24). The future life of our final consummation, the completion and perfection of our humanity and our fulfilment as persons, is already present in a partial or hidden way in our Christian experience.

In the end, we believe in the new life of the world to come because we experience newness of life already in the present. 'The hour is coming, and now is, when the dead will hear the voice of the Son of God, and those who hear will live' (*John* 5:25). The transcendent God who has already graciously changed and renewed our lives can be relied upon to continue the good work that has begun in us to change us and perfect us and make us new in his heavenly kingdom beyond the veil of death.

We believe in eternal life, because the interpenetration of historical time and the future of God's eternity is something of which we have some experience already – we know ourselves to be 'the children of the resurrection'. And every eucharist is a time when with all the saints of God and all Christian souls we join in the one divine communion of love and peace, which is the foretaste of eternal life of God the Holy Trinity – Father, Son and Holy Spirit.

15

WHATEVER HAPPENED
TO OSCAR MIDDLETON?

PREACHED IN ST GEORGE'S CATHEDRAL, PERTH,
ON EASTER DAY, 3 APRIL 1994.

Whatever happened to Oscar Middleton?

Oscar Middleton disappeared a few days ago although this was not reported in the Western Australian press. Oscar Middleton had been walking in Mount Street, West Perth right outside my front gate. Presumably he was doing nothing more than ambling nonchalantly around, minding his own business, enjoying the surroundings and disturbing nobody.

Then suddenly, unexpectedly and astonishingly, he was no longer there. He disappeared, but not entirely without trace – for he left behind a tell-tale clue, a sign right outside my house that he had been there. And the clue he left behind is what alerted us all to the mystery of his disappearance.

Oscar Middleton left behind a collar, which previously had been worn around his neck. There it was, lying forlornly in the middle of the footpath, waiting to be picked up – as it turned out by an American visitor to Perth – but Oscar himself was nowhere to be seen.

Fortunately the collar had a little tinkly bell and a tag attached to it. It was the tag, indeed, that provided the index to his identity: 'Oscar Middleton', it said, plus an address and contact phone number. On the back of the tag was the phone number of his vet in case of emergency. Presumably Oscar Middleton is a superior sort of cat, a pale grey Siamese perhaps, for it is usually only very superior Seal Points that wear red leather collars like this one.

And the question posed by the finding of this empty collar is, 'What became of Oscar Middleton and by what mysterious means did he disappear?'

Did he simply slip his head through the collar as through a noose and shake himself free of it in order to escape to feral freedom? Or did some person take a liking to him and remove the collar before spiriting him away? But if so, why was the collar still left done up? Worse still, did he encounter some gross and more aggressive animal which took him off to a sinister and tragic end?

Clearly, the mystery of the empty collar could only really be solved by checking things out. A phone call to his home number would be necessary to seek further information. But would we be breaking good news to his owner or bad? Well, happily, we were assured that he was in fact alive and well in the safety of his owner's protection and I parcelled up his collar and posted it back.

The mystery of the finding of the empty collar raised exactly the same kind of questions as the narrative story of the empty tomb, with the linen cloths lying as if Jesus had simply vanished from within them. This is a story that does not really answer questions. Indeed, it raises more questions than it answers. Did the distraught women mourners go back to the right tomb or to another nearby empty tomb by mistake? Was the body deliberately removed and spirited away to prevent the tomb from becoming the centre of continuing political agitation and dissent? Did Jesus revive spontaneously in the tomb, as a consequence of the effect of the embalming spices acting like smelling salts and then, as the nineteenth century liberal thinker Renan suggested, free himself from the tomb and go on to borrow the gardener's clothes?

Or is the account of the empty tomb not so much the ground of faith as a story which arose out of the faith of the early Christian community as it struggled to communicate an otherwise mysterious and spiritual kind of experience? Did an original account of the women returning to find the tomb get embroidered in the telling and retelling of it, so that it was embellished with accretions, such as additional numbers of women witnesses? The name of Mary Magdalene is the only name to feature consistently in all four Gospel records.

There is the reference in *Mark's Gospel* to an angel delivering an interpretative message like a news flash, 'Go into Galilee, there you will see him.' In *Matthew's Gospel* there's a reference to two angels who are more actively involved in rolling back the stone. Is the additional reference to soldiers standing guard at the tomb and being frightened by the earthquake that accompanied the angels' action a later addition to Mark's original story, which is without these details?

Alternatively, can the original Marcan story of the empty tomb itself be the residue of an early Christian liturgy? Do we detect echoes of that in the procession of the women at the early morning hour of Sunday worship? Is the empty tomb story the ground of faith or the product of faith – the basis of belief or a way of expressing it?

There are really no quick and easy answers to such questions, for at two thousand years remove, we simply do not have access to sufficiently concrete evidence to settle the matter one way or another. We cannot cross-examine and otherwise check out the witnesses. And a wise person, as the philosopher Hume once said, will always proportion his or her belief to the actual evidence. One can hardly just choose to opt for one explanation of the tomb story and then hold one's breath in the hope that one can sustain one's conviction in the absence of rational support by a sheer act of will.

So what precisely is the significance of the story for us in the celebration of our Easter faith?

Given the ambiguity of the narrative of the empty tomb, its continuing usefulness for us is precisely that it *does* raise questions. It is not so much a proof as a pointer, a sign which invites us to check out Christian claims by seeking further information. It alerts us to the mystery of the unexplained – the unexplained fact that we exist at all – and it raises in our consciousness the possibility of a life beyond the grave in the safety and protection of the God who created us.

However, our Easter faith is a matter, not so much of believing a particular interpretation of an historical narrative to be true, even despite a shortfall in the evidence, or of first believing that there is a God somewhere who has such and such a nature. Rather, it is a matter of encountering the energising presence of the unique Spirit that we in faith identify as the Spirit of Christ in the life of the Christian community. In other words, the empty tomb is once again not so much a proof as a pointer. It alerts us to the possibility of encountering the presence of the raised Christ in our own experience where two or three are gathered in unity of heart and mind, in the generosity and grace of human love and care, in the breaking of bread, in the inner voice of conscience, in the Word of address that stops us in our tracks and insistently calls us to discipleship, in the communion of persons one with another by mutual self-gift.

For what we experience in any authentically Christian community, if we care to check it out, is not a great emptiness but the personal presence of a particular and distinctive Spirit, a Spirit of love of a unique and specific kind to which the first Christians referred by conjuring up the word 'agape'. It is a self-giving which is remembered as first defined in the community that gathered around the unique human self who was Jesus – and that we find living still as the fluid extension, as it were, of his personality.

Just as the influence of any significant person, such as the leader or head of an association of persons, moves among the group to give it cohesion and identity, and whose energising presence is acknowledged, so we trace the unique self-giving or love, which is the inner-spiritual substance of the shared community life and experience of Christians, to the unique centre of personality who is Jesus.

The message of Easter is that the unique self-giving that was defined in his words and work, his life of self-sacrifice and ultimately his death for others, was indeed *defined* in his historical existence, but not *confined* there. For we encounter it, living still as the energising Spirit of the Christian community. We therefore celebrate today the Resurrection of Christ as the ground of our own life beyond the grave because we already experience the new life in Him. 'I, yet not I,' as Paul says, 'the Spirit of Christ in me' (*Galatians* 2:20; *Romans* 8: 9–11).

The narrative story of the empty tomb is significant for us today, not as a proof, but because of its sign value. It raises for us a possibility and alerts us to a presence which, enfolding us in and through the loving care and support of our brothers and sisters in Christ, assures us of the ultimate love and care of the owner and protector of us all – and grounds the fundamental conviction that we are his people and he is our God.

16

SALT

PREACHED AT THE OPENING EUCHARIST OF THE SYNOD
OF THE DIOCESE OF PERTH ON 20 OCTOBER 1994, AT WHICH
WORSHIPPERS WERE PRESENTED WITH A LITTLE SACHET
OF SALT AS THEY ARRIVED.

Around 1992, I received a visit from a man who, when the appointment was made with my secretary, said that he needed some advice about immigration and permanent residence in Australia, and about setting up a business. He gave his name as Snobar. S–N–O–B–A–R. I think I was expecting somebody from Norway.

It turned out that he was a displaced Palestinian Christian who had been living with his wife and family in Amman. (Snobar is apparently a fairly common Arab name.) His wife was the daughter of a former Bishop of Jerusalem and the Middle East, and I guess this ecclesiastical link was the reason why they chose to call on me. They told me that they had already obtained permission to migrate to Australia, and were on a reconnaissance visit to Perth to determine whether or not they could establish a viable branch of their business in

Western Australia. It was about the future business that they really wanted advice from me.

I said that I would gladly help them settle in Perth and asked them about their business. To my astonishment, the business for which they sought advice had to do with the marketing of salt. But this was not just any salt, but salt mined on the shores of the Dead Sea which is, of course, unusually salty. Mr Snobar held one of only two or three local government licences for the gathering of salt at the Dead Sea, which his business packaged and sold as 'bath salts'. When I asked the Snobars why they thought Australians might be interested in bathing in Dead Sea salt, they pointed out that these were natural, unperfumed bath salts, and that they could be expected to have a unique appeal in an environmentally correct way.

I was not able to give them much help about Dead Sea bath salts, but I did give them some advice about purchasing a house in Perth and what suburbs they might look at so as to be close to a church school for their children. They were happy enough with that and left, and I heard nothing more from them. Perhaps their own market research was not too encouraging; perhaps the dramatic changes for the good in Israeli/Palestinian relations at the time meant that the pressure to migrate was not so intensely felt. Then a couple of years ago the delightful Snobars turned up as members of a local parish. When I asked about the business they said they were into computers!

At any rate I still have, sitting at the end of the bath, a complimentary packet in an orange, yellow and black striped drawstring bag labelled 'Dead Sea Bath Salts'. This is a regular reminder to me, not just of the Dead Sea, Palestine, and the Snobars, but also of the Gospel saying about salt, 'You are the salt of the world.' For our Lord's reference to salt is almost certainly geographically connected with the Dead Sea, the most prolific source of salt in the Holy Land in his day, as it still is in ours.

Given the biblical reference of today's Gospel (*Mark* 9: 42–9), I am now tempted to open the Snobar's bag of natural salt crystals and taste them to determine whether or not, after all this time, the salt has lost its flavour. For it strikes me as odd that salt should be thought to have a shelf-life. The little packets of salt with which you have been furnished carry no use-by date. Indeed, the more I think about Jesus talking about salt losing its saltiness, the stranger it becomes. After all, salt in the ancient world, apart from being used to give added flavour to cooking, was valuable as a preservative. In the days before modern refrigeration salt was so valuable as a preservative that it was often used as currency. People in the Roman world would be recompensed for their labour, not just with cash but with a regular bag of salt, hence the term 'salary'. If salt itself is a preservative, isn't it somewhat odd to suggest that over time it could lose its saltiness?

Perhaps Our Lord was speaking of a theoretical, notional possibility, rather than of something that might actually happen. Perhaps he meant that bland cooking can be livened up with a pinch of salt but if the salt itself were to become bland, what would season the salt?

Whatever the exact meaning of that statement, that is not the end of the story. Mark gives a slight twist to the 'you are the salt of the world' saying. That is actually Matthew's version of the text. Mark has, 'Salt is good, but if the salt has lost its saltiness, how will you season it? Have salt in yourselves and be at peace with one another.'

'Have salt in yourselves.' In literal terms, of course, that is hardly good advice. My wife is constantly telling me that salt is not good, and that I put too much salt into myself. In fact, she says that it could be the death of me rather than something life-enhancing and good. When Jesus said that salt was good and advised his disciples to have salt in themselves, he was surely speaking metaphorically, exhorting them to vitality in their Christian life rather than a bland and flavourless life of mediocre commitment. In other words they were to be at pains to avoid the charge that is so often levelled at us Anglicans – the charge of being the bland leading the bland! By having salt in us and by being salt to the world we can contribute to the quality of life in the world – to revitalise it and give it a distinctive flavour, the flavour of eternity.

In all this we have a clue to understanding our relationship as Christians with the world. At the beginning of the decade of evangelism in the 1990s we became increasingly conscious of the need to develop new-member ministries. In order to grow congregations we needed to develop strategies to ensure that people were welcomed and cared for and integrated into the life of the Church. We needed to avoid the experience of having them come in the front door and disappear out through the back door! Getting more people into the life of the Church by evangelism might, indeed, be thought to be the chief thrust of our mission in the world.

But the message of the salt is a little different. For it is not the purpose of salt to try to turn the stew into more salt. Rather, it is there to heighten the vitality and the flavour of the stew. There is a parallel in Jesus' saying about the leaven in the lump. The role of yeast in dough is not to turn the dough into more yeast, but to distribute itself through the dough to lighten its texture and fluff it out of its heaviness.

Perhaps the Church's chief purpose and role, as a minority ingredient in society, is to give life and flavour to the whole, raising up and transforming the quality of it, rather than trying to turn more of the world into the Church.

Of course, if we do our work of service well, with enthusiasm and vitality, there will be a proportion of the world that will respond to the invitation to join us in our mission. Evangelism will go hand in hand with our ministry of service and care; by our fruits we will be known and others will want to join in the work of transforming the world. But the role of the Church is primarily to serve the world rather than to serve its own interests by getting a bit more of the world into the pews.

To think otherwise is to fall into the Constantinian fallacy. This is the fallacy of yearning to recreate the position of the Church as it was early in the fourth century when, after the conversion of Constantine, to be a citizen of the Empire was to be a Christian, just by being born into it; and to be a Christian was co-terminus with being a citizen of the Empire. By contrast, our calling may be to live in the world as a minority movement, as a minor ingredient in a greater whole. It may well be that it is God's intention that we shall always be so, but called to work for the whole as the salt of the world.

In his journals the Danish existentialist thinker Soren Kierkegaard often distinguished between being salt and being just part of the crowd. For Kierkegaard, to be salt is to resist being neutralised by the world; to be in the world, serving the world but not being drawn into it in such a way as to take on its values and accommodate oneself to its standards of behaviour. Even the highest standards of behaviour, such as living a reasonably decent life or being a paragon of civic virtue, fall short of the Christian ideal. That, indeed, is precisely when salt loses its savour. And in relation to this, Kierkegaard points to Mark's preceding verse to the call to 'have salt in yourselves'.

It reads, 'Everyone will be salted with fire' (*Mark* 9.49) and some ancient texts go on to read 'and every sacrifice will be salted with salt'. For Mark, fire, sacrifice and salt go together. Can it be that, if one gives oneself unconditionally, genuinely and passionately serving others, it follows that one will necessarily suffer oneself to be consumed as a sacrifice to God? Such a commitment will involve loving mercy, doing justice and walking humbly, but not without fire in one's belly. To be salt not crowd means to preserve one's radical Christian identity so as to bring it to the transformation of the otherwise flavourless whole.

We all know that it is only too easy to use our religion as nothing more than bath salts – to become languid and passive, and to be soothed as we lie back and luxuriate in it. We allow our religion to work on us as a cosmetic, as a superficial addition to a life of uneventful blandness.

Even worse, we can use our religious commitment as a kind of preservative, you might say as the brine of life. As a kind of pickling solution in which we immerse ourselves so as to 'preserve our bodies and souls unto everlasting life' (as the 1662 service had it). We can become essentially inert, self-involved and lacking in vitality, drive and purpose – just hanging on to a very bland, domesticated kind of life, serving time until our own use-by date comes up.

It is in the face of this kind of very real alternative that we hear again Jesus' words as a Word of address to us, 'Have salt in yourselves!'

17

TELESCOPES, MICROSCOPES, AND PERISCOPES

PREACHED AT THE CONSECRATION OF PHILIP JAMES
HUGGINS AS ASSISTANT BISHOP OF THE DIOCESE OF PERTH,
ON 2 FEBRUARY 1995. A SECOND PRESENTATION OF SIMILAR
THOUGHTS WAS PREACHED AT THE OPENING EUCHARIST
OF THE ELECTORAL SYNOD OF THE ARCHDIOCESE
OF MELBOURNE ON 24 FEBRUARY 2000.

Telescopes, microscopes, and periscopes obviously have something in common. They are all to do with seeing, whether seeing far-off things up close, or seeing tiny things much much larger than life, or seeing all around with unimpeded vision, over the top of a crowd, or above the level of the sea if one happens to be at the periscope of a submarine.

It may not be so obvious that these various instruments of seeing also have something in common with bishops. For the English word 'bishop' is a translation of *episkopos*, from the Greek word *epi* meaning 'over' and *skopos* meaning 'seer'. A bishop is literally an *epi-skopos*, an over-seer.

So apart from saying something this evening relating to the consecration of an over-seer, I also want to say something about some other ways of seeing that are integral to being a bishop that are suggested by telescopes, microscopes, and periscopes. Indeed, apart from consecrating an *episkopos*, or *epi-skopos*, he will in days ahead, become equally a *tele-skopos, micro-skopos and peri-skopos*. Let me explain what I mean.

First, in order to focus upon what is involved in the particular form of oversight appropriate to a bishop, we are usually content to unpack the meaning content of the biblical image of the shepherd. We place in a bishop's hand a shepherd's crook as a reminder that his over-sight involves the care and protection of the flock.

Moreover, as we all learned at Sunday school, in the ancient world shepherding necessarily involved leadership, for prior to the enclosure of paddocks with fences, the flock wandered from pasture to pasture, following the shepherd, and responding instinctively to his call. Indeed, if your preparation for Confirmation was up to scratch, you will remember that it was important for the shepherd to go before as leader and for the sheep to follow, otherwise he might get confused with the one who comes up from behind, and that would be a complete disaster, for the one who comes from behind is, of course, the butcher!

But, it is important to be aware that the biblical shepherding imagery illuminates only one, somewhat limited aspect of what is involved in episcopal ministry. We must enlarge its scope.

The word *episkopos* is used in the New Testament itself quite independently of the imagery of the shepherd. *1 Timothy* 3: 1–7, for example, sets out the fundamental qualities required of a bishop. Anyone who aspires to the office of oversight must be above reproach, married only once, temperate, sensible, dignified, hospitable, an apt teacher, no drunkard, not violent but gentle of disposition, not quarrelsome, and no lover of money. The passage goes on to say that he must manage his own household well, for if a person does not manage his own household well, 'how can he care for God's Church?'

This means we should not necessarily conjure up the image before our mind's eye of the antique shepherd of the nursery rhyme book, in felt hat, smock and holding a crook, and then picture the bishop's ministry in the form of a kind of bucolic chumminess involving a leisurely and passive surveillance of the flock. That rather romantic and rural image is certainly not what the more urbanised Timothy had in mind. Indeed, it is as well to remember that Christianity very quickly became an urban movement in the ancient world, a religion of cities and a primary catalyst of civilisation. It was the pagans, unsophisticated yokels who, as the term 'pagan' suggests, were *de la campagne*, from the country.

It is not surprising then that Timothy's Church is not so much the flock as the household of faith, and his *episkopos* essentially a household manager, whose oversight is much more akin to that of the modern business administrator or company manager than we might think. It is not for nothing that our prayer book speaks of the consecration of a bishop as an admission to government in the Church.

Moreover, the antecedents of the New Testament word *episkopos* already carry a similar set of nuances. Whether in essentially Jewish texts or in the surrounding secular and religious culture of the ancient Greek world, it is used as a technical name for public administrative officials, inspectors and financial controllers. And there are some Syrian inscriptions that record that an *episkopos* was the overseer of building construction sites.

So my first point is this. We must not romanticise the kind of oversight that pertains to the role of a bishop by concentrating exclusively on an antique rural image of the shepherd, and then wring our hands because bishops in the dioceses of the modern cities of the western world do not conform to something approximately to this narrowly pastoral stereotype.

Bishops need not feel that they must apologise for failure to conform to it; still less need we agonise and become neurotic because, try as we may, we do not seem to be able to actualise it.

And certainly, while an assistant bishop's work in the burgeoning northern suburbs of this city will involve the pastoral care of clergy and people within his immediate area of responsibility as a top priority, it will involve much more. Indeed, before there is a flock to which to be the shepherd, there will be strategies for Church growth to be developed, outreach to be organised, the work of agencies of care to be coordinated, parishes to be planted, budgets to be balanced and funds to be raised and administered. And if we are to keep to our target of forty new parishes by the end of the 1990s, not to mention the eventual building of Grace Cathedral at Joondalup, he will probably find himself not infrequently wearing the hard hat of the overseer on a construction site.

But, if the bishop's role is one of oversight in this broad and complex sense, there is also a sense in which he is, in addition to being *episkopos*, a *tele-skopos*. For one of the bishop's roles is to bring what is far-off near, so that we see it close up, as it were. He brings the distant end or *telos* close to hand, so that we feel that we can almost reach out and touch it. For the bishop is a sign of the Church's continuity through time, standing in an unbroken succession of apostolic faith and values from the Church of the Apostles.

We have the very erudite seventeenth century Irish bishop, James Ussher, to thank for our contemporary perception at this point. This was the same Bishop Ussher who calculated that the earth was created at 9 a.m. in the morning one day in 4004 BC. But his theological legacy is more enduring than his quaint mathematical calculations, for it was Bishop Ussher who in the seventeenth century rediscovered and translated in the Christian West the letters of St Ignatius of Antioch.

Before the ink of the New Testament was dry – perhaps before some of it was even written – we know from Ignatius that the bishop was being seen as president of the eucharistic community and the focus of its unity. 'Wherever the bishop is, there is the Church' and 'without the bishop the name of Church is not given.' The bishop is the sign of authentic Christian community against the sectarianism of those who at the slightest provocation or disagreement want to hive off to do their own thing.

This soon came to be developed into the idea of the bishop as the sign of continuity with the Church of the past. As teacher and guardian of the deposit of scripture and the apostolic tradition, the bishop's role is to focus attention upon faith's ancient norms, magnify them and bring them close to hand, particularly when the Church under his care is in danger of straying away from them.

But that does not mean that he brings the past into the present as a kind of straitjacket of a restrictively cloying and life-denying kind. The Church's tradition is a living tradition and her voice a living voice. The tradition of faith does not just come to us as a heavy dead weight, like so many glassy-eyed fish on a fishmonger's marble slab. Rather, what is received from the past has to be made our own and re-expressed in the language of today. And very importantly, it has to be brought to bear on the issues of today, the truths of faith being like very lively and elusive fish yet to be hooked and drawn into our baskets of understanding. We live *into* the tradition as much as *out* of it. And this means that the bishop is thus a sign of continuity with the Church of the future as much as of the past. For part of the bishop's role of leadership has to do with moving the Church forward towards its true *telos* or end, into a fuller perception of truth.

Moreover, one of the far-off images that, as *tele-skopos*, or end-seer, he brings near to hand is the image of the Church of the future. A very distinguished contemporary Greek Orthodox theologian, John Zizioulas, has pointed out that Ignatius of Antioch's original image of the Church assembled around the bishop in unity and peace is not a description of the Church as it ever originally was, so much as an ideal image of the Church as by grace it can and should become. It was in the face of disunity and threat of division that Ignatius held up the ideal of the one eucharistic community of the city gathered in unity around the bishop, catholic or inclusive of all the baptised in that place, and living in perfect harmony and peace.

The bishop as *teleskopos* is a sign of continuity with the coming great Church of the future as much as of the past, the eucharistic community gathered around him being an anticipation of the perfect human community of peace and love of the eschatological end-time, when Christ shall be all in all.

As the bishop of today and the community gathered around him struggle to actualise that, two ends meet: the Church's alpha and omega. The apostolic beginnings and the eschatological end and goal are brought into closer range, as it were.

Apart from being *epi-skopos* and *tele-skopos*, the bishop is *micro-skopos*. He does not only oversee the life of the flock of Christ and manage the affairs of the household of faith in some broad and detached sense, and constitute a sign of continuity with the Church both of the past and of the future. At the same time, he attends to the little things of life of individual clergy and of particular parishes, themselves the microcosms and sub-centres that together comprise the diocesan whole.

As we think of the bishop as the *micro-skopos*, the small-seer, the image of the shepherd may be usefully reintroduced, for the ancient shepherd's intimate relation to the flock who responded to his voice also entailed that he himself in turn knew them all by name. Indeed, he counted them into the protective enclosure of the fold one by one each evening, as we do in our prayers, noting the absence of any unaccounted-for or wayward individual and taking the appropriate redemptive action for the recovery of the lost.

A bishop's visitation to a parish will often involve microscopic attention and much precise listening and discernment, so as to put a finger on what may be going wrong and to help eliminate the occasional bug in the parish pathology and refocus the mission. This means that the bishop oversees, but not just in a removed, detached and macrocosmic way while dealing with the big picture. It is this that distinguishes him radically from the captains and leaders of the modern world of commerce and industry.

Moreover, it is to allow for the flowering of really genuine pastoral care that assistant bishops become so necessary, and why the diocese is divided into regions of not more than fifty or so parishes. Matters of manageable scale are important so that a bishop does not get swamped by the demands of the large picture, with no time to attend effectively to micro structures. As *microskopos*, he attends to small things as though they were large, and takes responsibility for an episcopal region as though it were a diocese in its own right, lest episcopal oversight should overlook the little things of life, where small is beautiful.

And finally, he is *peri-skopos*. Given all that he has to do, a bishop must necessarily develop the ability to lift his line of vision above the crowd so as to see more clearly all round, to glimpse again the vision of God in clearer air, and grasp once more the vision of man and woman not as they are but as God can make them.

Paul Tillich once said that 'whenever humans encounter the ultimate they tend to seek refuge in the preliminaries'. Fussing about unimportant things and not being able to see beyond the wood for the trees is endemic in all human communities. And one becomes one-eyed if one stays at the microscope too long. For every Christian it is the entry into prayerful and reflective space that alone allows us to rise above all this so as to see more as God sees; that is to say to see periscopically all round with unimpeded vision.

And it is the bishop's sometimes difficult task to try to lift the sights of the community as a whole by kindling dreams and raising possibilities lest the Church gathered around him should become submerged and drown in the unimportant minutiae of life. As the prophet of wisdom says, 'without a vision the people perish' (*Proverbs* 29:18). He cannot do that unless he himself has time for access to the periscope of prayer for the contemplative engagement with the divine that allows us all to rise above it all.

A bishop is *episkopos*, *teleskopos*, *microskopos* and *periskopos*. At least that is the way I see it. I invite you to see it that way too.

18

PROGRESS IN RELIGION

PREACHED IN ST GEORGE'S CATHEDRAL, PERTH ON THE
FEAST OF PENTECOST, 4 JUNE 1995.

A few weeks ago Paul Davies, Adelaide University's Professor of Mathematical Physics, was in London to be presented with the Templeton prize for Progress in Religion by the Duke of Edinburgh. The Templeton Prize is one of a number of awards sponsored by the now 83-year-old Sir John Templeton, a devout American Presbyterian who, after being educated at Yale and later at Oxford, made his fortune on Wall Street. He now spends his time administering it and distributing its income to worthy religious causes.

And quite a fortune it must be. Last year he gave away $14 million; this year it is $16 million, and next year it is anticipated to be $20 million. Professor Paul Davies' prize for progress in religion is worth $1.4 million. It was awarded by a panel of judges, including former United States president, George Bush, a devout Anglican and one-time church warden, former British prime minister, Margaret Thatcher, and seven other judges who determined that Professor Davies should receive the prize for his work on black holes, time and the beginning of the universe, and his many publications in which he argues for the mathematical improbability of it all being a random happening of mere chance.

There is a certain awesome elegance, he says, about the mathematical calculations of physical astronomy and this speaks to him of the 'mind of God' (the title of his most widely known book). The idea that physical matter somehow made itself seems to Professor Davies just too hard to swallow.

Certainly, his physicist's talk of the 'mind of God' as it is expressed through the regularities of nature, were reckoned by the judges to have breached the barrier between science and religion. So 'well done' to an Australian physicist. I guess the message in this for all of us is to get our heads down and make progress in religion, for this prize is larger than any of the Nobel prizes and up in the Lotto league and who knows who will get it next?

What interested me about the press coverage of this event, which I happened to see originally in the *Sydney Morning Herald*, was first the journalist's puzzlement concerning the motivation behind Sir John Templeton, a hard-headed financier, in awarding prizes and funding research projects on matters related to religion. Why should a businessman be so interested in religion as to give his money away to it?

But what the *Sydney Morning Herald* reporter found even more intriguing was the idea of offering a prize, not just for promoting peace (for there is a Templeton Prize for religious people who make significant contributions to peace) but a prize precisely for *progress* in religion.

Religion, after all, is more often than not thought to be something that focuses on the past: past religious leaders, a received set of scriptural truths from the past, a doctrinal and liturgical tradition to be preserved in the face of all the 'changes and chances of this fleeting world'. Indeed, the adherents of religion are more often than not cast as reactionaries rather than progressively minded people.

The *Sydney Morning Herald* journalist himself noted that the idea of a prize for progress in religion seems in some respects a curiously nineteenth century one. In that century it seemed that the world was driven by 'progress'. It appeared to be gradually becoming a better place, inexorably evolving towards a more peaceful, civilised and morally perfect society. Science was notching up one remarkable discovery after another. Medicine had discovered bacteria and anaesthetic; steam trains were opening up possibilities for travel hitherto unknown; the 'untamed native' tribes were being civilised and the Gospel brought to them by the burgeoning missionary societies of the time. It looked as though human progress in almost every field would operate as an internal drive to bring the world to a better place.

This self-confidence was shattered by World War I, which suddenly put an end to nineteenth century talk of 'progress'. And the horrors of successive wars and increasing violence – racial, soccer, domestic – to apparently mindless violence, have only gone to underline for us the illusory nature of the naive view that the world is somehow becoming better.

Moreover, the idea of progress *in religion*, of all things, seemed to the *Sydney Morning Herald* writer something of an oddity. He wrote:

> The idea that spiritual knowledge can make progress, so that this year's doctrines are superior to those of last century is not popular among religions at the moment, when fundamentalism seems to provide the only vigour.

In other words, this journalist was challenged by the view that progress *can* be made in religious thinking and religious knowledge because religion, for him at least and, I suspect, many other people in our world, seemed to be about the preservation of past truth. The religious fundamentalist, in particular, whether Christian, Muslim or Hindu, seems committed to the rabid and unbending defence of a received set of truths, rather than a more open and adventurous entry into a yet-to-be-discovered truth of the future. So Professor Davies' prize for progress in religious thought seemed to the *Sydney Morning Herald* journalist almost a contradiction in terms.

What struck me about this perception of religion was just how wrong it is, at least from an authentically Christian point of view.

True, some of the more conservative approaches to religious truth on both sides of the Catholic/Protestant divide have given the impression that all the truths of the faith have been once and for all delivered to the saints. Papal statements are said to be infallible and irreformable, an absolute expression of the mind of God received from on high and therefore not subject to revision and change, let alone correction by somebody else. The more right-wing sixteenth century Protestant reformers spoke of revelation as something that happened in the past, which was completed at the 'death of the last of the apostles'. They believed that this revelation then got fossilised and enshrined in an absolute kind of way in scripture. At that point God's revelation was understood to be finished. Thereafter, it was argued, the Holy Spirit illuminated the reader to allow him or her to understand and appropriate its truths in personal life, but there could be no further revelation.

This distinction between revelation and illumination was in fact an invention of the reformers. The New Testament itself always speaks of revelation, not as something past and finished, but as the full disclosure of the truth of Christ that will occur on the Day of the Lord, the final day of all history, when we shall know even as we are known. Truth for New Testament Christians was an eschatological reality, a reality belonging to the end-time. Christ's promise of the Holy Spirit that we celebrate today is precisely that the Spirit will *lead* us into all truth.

True, Jesus Christ is for Christians the ultimate and final revelation of God, but we await his appearing. Meanwhile, the Spirit is the first fruits of an anticipated greater harvest to come, or the down payment or guarantee of what awaits us when dividends are calculated and a final payout is made, as Paul would say. The full disclosure of the truth of God for Christians lies in the future, and any grasp of truth we are admitted to in this world is not fixed and absolute, but provisional in the literal sense of that word. 'Provisional' means literally 'pro-visional', that is 'before the vision', before the clarity of vision of the end-time, prior to the Lord's return and the full revealing of the good purposes of God. Meanwhile, all our insights are subject to revision and require re-expression and constant refinement.

New Testament Christianity is thus a future-oriented religion that hopes and prays for the fulfilment of the promises of God, the return of the Lord and the perfect disclosure of the reign of God in justice and peace. That is why we daily pray 'your kingdom come'. 'Beloved, it does not yet appear what we shall be' (*1 John* 3:2).

The very word 'revelation' in Greek bears this future-centred colouring, for the Greek word for 'revelation' is *apokalypsis*, something disclosed ultimately only at the apocalypse, the end of time. Meanwhile, we must be content to see 'as through a glass dimly', as Paul says, not face to face.

The clarity of face to face encounter with the truth of God in Christ is a reality of the future.

So the idea of progress in religion, which suggests that this year's doctrines may be superior to those of the past, is certainly not alien to the Christian mentality. The development of doctrine and the constant reformation of received views at the insistent prompting of the Holy Spirit are part and parcel of the adventure into God.

This does not mean, of course, that the remembered past is unimportant. The norms of scripture and the doctrinal insights of the ancient fathers and mothers of the Church and the ancient creeds are precious to us. As the German poet Goethe said: 'He who does not draw on three thousand years, is living from hand to mouth.' But we draw on the riches of scripture and tradition, not as destinations in their own right but as pointers on the way.

We have, after all, long since abandoned a fundamentalist pseudo-scientific reading of *Genesis* where, impossibly, light is said to be created on the first day *before* the Sun and Moon, which were created only on the fourth day. We have long since abandoned a biblical cosmology where the earth is understood to be the centre of our universe rather than the sun. Professor Davies' re-expression of a doctrine of creation, in which purpose rather than randomness is understood to be disclosed mathematically in the scientifically determined physical regularities of nature, is but a further refinement of the impact of the reflections of Galileo and Copernicus and others of the world of science who have gone before.

All this means that with the promise of the Spirit to lead us into all truth we can understand ourselves as a people who move into a largely unknown future, with the insights of our religious past to build on. Guided by the norms of scripture, our doctrinal tradition and our God-given reason, we set out on a journey of discovery in faith and hope. And this future-centred orientation is perhaps very much in our mind in this particular week of the year, not just because it is Pentecost, but because we celebrate at this time, on 6 June, the foundation of our state of Western Australia, and naturally think of what lies ahead of us as we give thanks for the inheritance of the past. We think of progress, not just in religion, but in every other possible kind of way.

But this kind of progress is not just a nineteenth century style of self-confidence in a drive to bring the world inexorably to a better place. We do not, in naive optimism, overlook the tragedy of the world. Rather, our hopes are for the good things of the promised kingdom of God of which the gift of the Spirit and the human harmony and peace it creates among us is promise and down payment. And these good things of the kingdom of God call in question the world as it is and make us dissatisfied with it, and thus prompt us to work actively for its reformation and improvement – for justice, human reconciliation and peace. We do not just place our hope naively in what might be called 'human progress'. What we hope for is grounded in God's promise, for the gift of the Spirit of love that is poured out in our hearts is itself both anticipation and promise of what is possible for all humanity in time to come. The Holy Spirit is the promise of progress and it calls in question a good deal of what in the world masquerades as progress.

Indeed it is from this perspective that we Christians hear the voice of John F. Kennedy, who liked to quote some famous words of George Bernard Shaw:

> Some people look at the sorry state of this present
> world and shake their heads and ask 'Why?' Others
> look to the world of the future and ask 'Why not?'

19

THE SPIRIT OF ATTENTIVENESS

PREACHED AT THE GENERAL THEOLOGICAL SEMINARY
OF THE EPISCOPAL CHURCH OF THE UNITED STATES OF AMERICA,
NEW YORK CITY, ON ASH WEDNESDAY, 21 FEBRUARY 1996.

During a visit to Italy a few years ago I was privileged to spend one weekend in Assisi, the romantic little city perched on a high hill overlooking the very spacious valley of Umbria, which in the early thirteenth century produced St Francis. As those of you who have been there will know, Assisi is still very much as it originally was. It is a town of charming little pink and white stone houses lining narrow, crooked streets. Because of the association of many of its churches with St Francis himself, it is a very popular stopping place for bus-loads of tourists who are regularly hurried into the centres of interest and out again, before being pushed into a bus to be taken on to the next attraction. In the tourist season Assisi has a touch of the frantic about it.

On the site of the tomb of St Francis itself there is a splendid white-stone basilica. It was erected very shortly after St Francis' death and burial in honour of the local saint, but not without some controversy. Some of the Franciscan brothers felt at the time that it was all too lavish and grand, and quite out of keeping with the message of simplicity and poverty for which St Francis himself had stood.

In any event, the basilica was completed very quickly. Today it is, in effect, a double storey church because the spacious crypt under the main nave has been decorated and turned into a second place of worship. In both churches, the upper and lower, the walls and ceilings are similarly decorated with frescoes by Cimabue and Giotto. Those in the upper church are the very famous ones by Giotto depicting scenes from the life of St Francis that appear over and over in books on medieval art. And it is perhaps these, more than the actual tomb of St Francis itself, that the tourists now flock to see. This often leaves the lower church free for worship while the crowds jostle for viewing space upstairs.

On one of the evenings when I was there, I was sitting for a few minutes at the back of the nave of the lower church in the late afternoon quiet after the last of the bus-loads of tourists had been ushered out and upstairs. The door opened, a shaft of light fell across the floor and I noticed a boy come in. I judged that he was Italian and about twelve years of age, and that he had not been in the place before. He quietly moved up the nave, looking carefully at the frescoes and closely examining the carved furnishings, particularly the pew ends.

This struck me at the time because it was in such sharp contrast to the approach of the groups of tourists who had just left. They looked interested enough yet somewhat flustered, bewildered, a little over-excited, perhaps anxious about not seeing whatever it was that they had been brought to see as their guides hurried them around the building with their all-too-brief potted commentaries. The boy had time to be more leisurely in his approach. He was wrapped in an all-absorbing and quiet interest. I do not think he even noticed that I was there. And when he came to the dark mahogany carved wood stalls of the friars around the apse behind the altar, he ran his finger around the carving as if to trace the line of the grain.

In contrast to the tourists, hurrying from this thing to the next, he was quietly taking in the atmosphere. He embodied a spirit of deep attentiveness. And that is what I would like you to focus your thoughts on as we commence this Lenten observance – the spirit of attentiveness.

As Christians one of the things that marks us out as different from our non-Christian friends and neighbours, is our desire to attend to the presence of God. They may in some way believe in God; we attend to God. We are those, if you like, who seek to immerse ourselves in the divine environment and to run our finger down the grain of God, the grain of the divine in the world.

We focus, for example, meditatively on the distinctive quality of the gracious love that was defined in Jesus and lifted up in awful beauty on the Cross. We attend to the unique quality of the loving fellowship that we now know most clearly in the eucharistic communion of the breaking and sharing of bread, but which we also glimpse in fragments and threads running through the texture of our lives in the world outside. In Lent, in the spirit of attentiveness, we examine that love closely, attend to it, cherish it, celebrate it and give thanks for it, so as to be in a position to invite others to see it and attend to it as we do. That is one of the basic things that authentic Christian being is about. It means not nodding our assent to a catalogue of abstract doctrines so much as attending to God and focusing on God's concrete presence in our lives, primarily as the Spirit of generous love.

And if there is point in observing the season of Lent, then one of its chief purposes is surely to invite us to develop and deepen the spirit of inner attentiveness. Simone Weil, the French spiritual writer, once said that 'prayer consists of attention'. It is paying attention to God and to the needs of one's neighbour.

That is why in Lent we make an extra effort. We take a little extra time. We make a point of arriving at church just a little earlier than we normally do so as to commit ourselves to attend quietly to God before the eucharist, or morning or evening prayer, or whatever. We take a little more time in order to attend more closely to God's presence.

And this exercise will become especially poignant over the next weeks as we concentrate our attention on the passion, death and resurrection of Jesus, that series of events that are so central to our understanding of the revelation of God. The grain of God comes so clearly to the surface in the life of the lowly one, the humble one, the one who is unjustly dealt with, maltreated and executed, but who remains unchangeably and steadfastly loving to the end and then rises in triumph to demonstrate the truth, as David Jenkins used to say, that 'you can't keep a good God down'.

As I think of the boy in the basilica at Assisi some famous words of Paul Tillich resurface in my mind with a new freshness. Paul Tillich went to the United States from Germany in order to escape the Nazi persecution between the wars. When I was a theological student at Trinity College in the University of Melbourne (1962–65) we all read his book, *The Shaking of the Foundations,* with great interest. It had been popularised by John Robinson in *Honest to God* where he focused on Tillich's imagery of 'depth'. 'God is found in the depths of things.' God is found in those things that concern us ultimately; he is met when we are deeply concerned. He is met when we are undistractedly attentive to ultimate things. He is not simply 'believed in' as a remote and transcendent figure of the sky high above us, so much as met as a spirit that stirs deep within our concern. This is probably because the spirit of deep absorption with what we have to do and whatever it might be – a piece of written text, the contemplation of a piece of art, a breathtaking sight in nature, the attentiveness of a child intently playing with blocks on a carpet – tends automatically to cut out the rest of the outside world. What absorbs us in a spirit of deep attentiveness has a certain timelessness about it; it opens us to a glimpse of eternity. The boy did not notice that I was there.

Certainly, it is when we pause in Lent in deeper attentiveness that we are able to cut out some of the rest of the world's concerns for a little while and thus draw nearer to God himself. We focus on the grain of God's love in our lives. We contemplate it, value it, cherish it. And in the process we become more fully and deeply absorbed in the mystery of it.

But we also attend to the particularity of it. We are, of course, aware of the distinctiveness of Jesus as the unique human person he was. We follow the thread of the events of his unique life insofar as we are able to discern them, and especially the quality of his self-giving, which is the primary reason for our remembering of him. We thus attend to the narrative of the passion, with the Cross as its centre, in all its graphic particularity.

And this is not just for the purpose of drawing some general abstract maxim from it about the value of sacrificing one's life for one's friends, though that is a conclusion that may be drawn from it.

For Jesus' death is not just an exemplification of the general or universal principle of the value of self-sacrifice.

Instead, it has value for us, precisely in its historical particularity. What is revealed in that particular series of events is, above all else, *Jesus'* self-giving, not self-giving generally. That is what we attend to and reflect upon and cherish during the season of Lent.

Indeed, it is precisely our attentiveness to the particularity of that self-giving that alerts us to the mystery of it. Like all unique and particular things, it tends to defy our attempts to describe it. Like the uniqueness of the taste of lychees or the smell of hot bitumen, so the particularity of Jesus' self-giving passes our ability to reduce it to a few prosaic words or a simple descriptive formula. Rather we have to rehearse the Jesus story, as a whole, and pay attention to it with all the incidents and episodes in which Jesus acted and reacted. To attend to the particularity of the Jesus story is to enter into the mystery of a self-giving that transcends our capacity to express. That should not prevent us from trying to say something, but we need to be aware of our human limitations and of the fact that all the books in the world that could be written will not exhaust the need for our continuing attentiveness to its particularity.

The unique self-giving of Jesus needs to be known by our attentiveness to the grain of God in the narrative of the Jesus story. But at the end of the day it needs to be known not just by description but by acquaintance.

We need to recognise its continuation in our lives in the present as something experienced, something with which we are acquainted despite the difficulty we have in expressing it in words. This is what the first disciples were trying to talk about and describe. So let us use the first moments of our observation of Lent to commit ourselves to the deepening of the spirit of attentiveness – attentiveness to the grain of God, in the life and death of Christ in the past, in our own life, and in the world in the present.

The alternative is to live and work, and even to minister as a kind of ecclesiastical tourist in the world, flitting hurriedly from one thing to another, pushed around by the external forces to which we willingly or unwittingly submit ourselves by whoever the guide may be who waves the flag and urges us on to the bus of life so as to be somewhere else. The alternative is to pass superficially through life, never pausing long enough to engage with the divine environment. Such a life will be found, sooner or later to be without depth, without ultimate concern – in a certain sense without God.

Let us then commit ourselves to prayer understood as a form of attentiveness – 'Prayer consists of attention'.

20

BORN AGAIN ANGLICANS

PREACHED AT THE GENERAL THEOLOGICAL SEMINARY
OF THE EPISCOPAL CHURCH OF THE UNITED STATES OF AMERICA,
NEW YORK CITY, ON ASH WEDNESDAY, 21 FEBRUARY 1996.

L ent is traditionally a time for giving up things. Indeed, I
can recall when I was a child that Lent was a regular time
for a good deal of adult talk about giving up smoking. And, if I
am honest about it, I think I originally thought that Ash
Wednesday was called Ash Wednesday because it was the day
for quitting and stubbing out the Camels.

Alternatively, Lent was a time for giving up alcohol or
chocolates or sugar in coffee or whatever. Certainly, the
traditional way of keeping Lent has often unwittingly
pandered to the human tendency to consign religion to the
realm of the trivial. We humans suffer from a constant
inclination for the token observance, the superficial and the
purely outwardly religious show that we regularly make of
things, and that the Ash Wednesday Gospel (*Matthew* 6: 1–6)
warns us against – when you fast do not do it for public show;
do so in secret.

These days, of course, people quit smoking not so much for the good of their souls as for the good of their bodily health; and the renunciation of chocolates and other sweet things is more likely to be dictated by considerations of shape than of souls. Indeed, the tyranny of cholesterol counts, carcinogens and blood pressure readings means that in a sense the whole of life has become a kind of low-grade, protracted Lenten discipline.

So I guess these days, while we may well observe some kind of Lenten discipline by giving up things, for Lent is after all a fast, we may choose to take on something, something additional to our normal routine. If we feel the urge to give up things, we may prefer, for example, to give up time and take on some prayerful reflection and attend to the deepening of our prayer – extra meditative time to enter more deeply into the meaning of the scriptural text for us.

These days the purpose of a Lenten observance will almost certainly be interpreted in catechetical and neo-catechetical terms. If Lent was originally a time for the catechetical instruction of those preparing for Easter baptism, it is for us today a kind of recapitulation of that, a neo-catechetical preparation for the renewal of our Easter faith, for the renewal of our baptismal vows. For those of us who are ordained, Lent is a time of preparation as well for the renewal of our ordination vows.

In a sense Lent is a time for all of us to be born again to our Christian profession and to the particular individuation of the life of discipleship to which we are called, whether as lay people, deacons, priests or bishops.

On one occasion when my wife and I were in New York, I became quite fascinated to sample some United States television religion. On a couple of evenings I found myself watching Mother Angelica's night show on Eternal Word television. Unfortunately the host nun was away at the time, apparently negotiating some satellite rights in Europe. In her absence, viewers were urged to pray for the success of her mission by a rather unconvincing and over-rehearsed Dominican, who took her place. He lectured his audience on the doctrine of the sacraments in bite-sized segments, punctuated alternately by Stations of the Cross and advertisements for self-improvement courses and Cadillacs.

The neighbouring channel provided an opportunity to get some first-hand experience of television evangelism with some of the more notable evangelists who have since fallen from grace, and their heavily made-up wives with eyelashes as false as their smiles.

On this channel viewers were regularly urged to pick up a telephone and dial a toll-free number in order to have a born-again experience with a telephone prayer partner. The television cameras panned across a line of beautiful prayer partners who were anxiously waiting to take down names and addresses. 'To be born again … all you have to do … is pick up your telephone and dial this toll-free number … and why not do it now?'

We Anglicans do not respond too positively to the packaging, but there is no doubting the reality of the life-transforming impact of the religious experience of being born again. The joyous enthusiasm of conversion, the sense of renewal of life and of new purpose and direction, the empowering gift of the Holy Spirit are clearly all real for born again people. Indeed, as you know, the experience of being born again is so real that those who have had it are able to date it and regularly return to it as *the* turning point in their lives. Naturally, it tends to act as a watershed between what is seen increasingly as a former life of corruption and wickedness and the new life in Christ of goodness and truth.

It is clear enough too, that often the born again experience is had at the expense of negating and devaluing all that has gone before it. This means negating not only the self-centred life we call sin from which the person has rightly turned away in conversion of life, but negating all former religious experience and former involvement in committed Christian community life as well. Indeed, all former Christian involvement and even Christian upbringing is often put down and written off as mere formality, purely outward religious training, perfunctory practice, all show, empty of the true experience of salvation and of the Spirit.

All this is a challenge to us Anglicans. And confronted by this kind of phenomenon I find myself asking what being born again might mean for us? What precise form of inward renewal can be real for us?

For starters we can honestly say if asked if we are born again, 'Yes, I am born again … and again and again and again and again.' For renewal of life is something for us that happens regularly, and particularly, of course, it is something that happens regularly each Lent. Renewal of life, conversion of life, is not just something that occurred once on a specific occasion at a datable time in the past. Rather, if the observance of Lent, especially when viewed from a neo-catechetical perspective, is a preparation for the Easter renewal of baptismal vows and the renewal of faith, then the experience of being born again thus occurs for us at least annually, but hopefully much more often.

And if being born again is for us an 'again and again' experience, and if instead of dating it once and for all in the past, we anticipate that it will happen again and again each

Lent and on into the future, it is unlikely that we shall feel the need to deny the reality and positive value of our Christian, and indeed authentically human, experience prior to the time when we first consciously made the Christian profession our own. Certainly, for us, being 'born again' does not involve the denial of a significant segment of our former religious life as empty formality. Indeed, the programming of people to speak in such terms may strike us as somewhat puerile.

Perhaps you know the music of *Fiddler on the Roof* but have forgotten the details of the story. Let me call them forward from the recesses of your memory. The father of the Jewish family, the Fiddler Tevye, and his wife Golde, have the task of finding suitable husbands for their daughters, for marriages in their inherited culture have traditionally been arranged. In their parental eyes the most desirable young men would be those from families of good standing, with 'good prospects'; steady, short back and sides, hard-working young men – men of some potential substance, with an earning capacity, who could offer their daughters a secure home and a bright future.

But, one by one, each of the daughters comes to Tevye and tells him that she wants to marry, not a rich man, but somebody seemingly without prospects, somebody far less than financially substantial, but with whom she has nevertheless fallen madly in love.

The language of 'falling in love' is new to Tevye, for his marriage to Golde was an arranged one, organised for them both by their parents. But clearly the world is changing; romantic love is taking over. His daughters want to marry because they have fallen in love! What can he make of it?

Somewhat perplexed by all this, Tevye asks Golde, 'Golde, do you love me?'

Golde replies, 'Well, I share your bed don't I?'

'Yes,' says Tevye, 'but do you love me?'

'Well', she says, 'I bore all your children.'

'Yes, I know that, but do you love me?'

'Well,' says Golde, 'I wash your socks and underwear.'

'Yes,' says Tevye, 'but do you love me?'

Golde wonders what love can be if it is not the faithful carrying through of her wifely duties. But then she gives Tevye the answer he has been looking for. 'I don't know what love is,' she says, 'if it's not doing what we've done together over the years. But I can tell you this. If our marriage had not been arranged and I was in the position now of having to decide for myself, I surely would decide to marry you Tevye.'

In other words, even if it was not Golde's decision to marry Tevye in the first place, she can say that she would have wanted it to be as it has been and now is.

In a sense, that is what being born again means for us Anglicans. And it gives us our agenda for the keeping of Lent. For we may have been taken to baptism at six weeks of age, and been baptised with water and incorporated into the fellowship of the Spirit without our consciously knowing it. In a sense it may have all been arranged for us. We may have been sent off to Sunday School as a matter of course, and we may have been confirmed largely as a consequence of parental expectations – even to the point of being frog-marched up to the bishop for the laying on of hands. Perhaps we were confirmed because it was simply thought to be the right and proper thing to do. But our newfound experience of being born again is not a denial of that which has gone before, even if it was arranged for us. Rather, the experience of being born again is the experience of saying, 'If I had been in the position of deciding for myself, I would have said then as I say now,

"Yes" to all that.' I make my Christian profession my own. Instead of denying the value of all that lies on the other side of the divide, in our experience of being born again we accept what was decided for us as a decision of our own. That is something that as Anglicans we do not do just once, but again and again. And Lent, in particular, is the time for us to enter very intentionally into the process of preparation for that to happen. We review and reaffirm our faith commitment and make it our own, repent of any behaviour that is incongruent with it, and call down the transforming presence of the Spirit of love in our lives – again and again.

I suppose there are times when, for all of us, what we do becomes a matter of course, a duty. Perhaps there are some of us for whom the path to ordination was entered into as much because of the expectations and even the decisions of others when we honestly think about it. Perhaps it seemed the right and appropriate thing to do at the time, the next almost programmed thing to do after being an altar server, an organist, a reader, a member of the parish council. Perhaps, indeed, once we got ourselves into a training process in a seminary, ordination resulted almost automatically, to be followed by a succession of appointments of a fairly predictable kind.

It is precisely when we acknowledge that our life and work has become something of a routine that we can in Lent prepare ourselves to hear again the words similar to those of the Easter Christ to Peter:

> 'Do you love me?' 'Of course, you know that I love you. I have been with you from the beginning.' 'Yes,' says our Lord, 'feed my sheep. But do you love me?' 'Yes, you know that I love you. I am here aren't I; I am

regularly present at your supper – to share the bread and drink the cup with you. You know that I love you.' 'Yes,' says our Lord, 'tend my sheep. But do you love me?' 'Of course, I am committed to your work; I am working harder than at any time in my life. You can see by what I do that I love you.' 'Yes,' says our Lord, 'tend my lambs. But do you love me? Do you truly love me?'

The answer will be a renewed and renewing 'Yes, I love you' if we can say that, given the possibility of living our lives again, and in the light of all that has happened, we can indeed say 'Yes'; this is what I would have done and wanted to do if it had been in my power alone to decide and make it so.

Let us in Lent take the opportunity to review and reaffirm our baptismal commitments and our dedication to the solemn vocation to which we are called. And say our 'Yes' to the life that Providence has arranged for us and to which our Saviour, Lord and Christ calls us eternally – again and again.

21

WONTONS AND RAVIOLI

PREACHED IN ST GEORGE'S CATHEDRAL, PERTH
ON CHRISTMAS DAY, 25 DECEMBER 1996.

There is in the bottom of our refrigerator the remains of a packet of wonton skins. You can buy them at the Lucky Emporium in Brisbane Street, Northbridge, and I guess at other specialty Chinese food stores elsewhere in the world. I wonder if they are all as inaccessible as Brisbane Street which, as you may know, is a one-way street.

I didn't know what wonton skins were until last Saturday evening when I saw a very large number of them laid out on the kitchen workbench.

A wonton skin is a little square, about nine centimetres by nine centimetres, of thinly rolled stiff pastry made, I suspect, of rice flour. I watched last Saturday as a prawn, a mussel, a few small pieces of fish and a scallop, were placed into the middle of each of these squares. Then the edge of the wonton skin was carefully painted with milk and a second skin was applied to the top. The edges were then pressed together with a fork and sealed to make a little flat packet of seafood.

I innocently and helpfully asked, as I observed this painstaking assembly line, whether the corners were going to be pinched together in a kind of ruffle at the top, for in my experience wontons at Chinese restaurants always look that way. 'No,' was my wife's firm reply in her 'don't interfere' voice, 'these little packets are left flat. The recipe is actually called seafood ravioli.'

I later found that these oversized squares of ravioli were boiled and served in a very delicious milky broth with chopped rosemary, sage and garlic chives. If anybody is anxious to try this, just send in a stamped self-addressed envelope and I am sure my wife will be pleased to provide you with the recipe.

What intrigued me about these packets made of wonton skins was the fact that they were used to create wonton ravioli. Now that is an odd combination, I thought. You might also be forgiven for thinking that wonton ravioli is curiously unseasonal at the present time. For many of us this is the time for traditional English and European fare: roast turkey and ham, Christmas pudding, brandy butter and mince pies. At this point you are probably asking yourself exactly what am I getting at?

In the Middle Ages, the Gospel stories underwent a certain amount of embroidery. Most representations of the Christmas crib show Mary and Joseph, with the Christ child in a manger overlooked by an ox and an ass. This is the way we regularly see the scene on Christmas cards and in stained glass windows. But in the Gospel story there is actually no mention of an ox and an ass. These are elements added in the course of the story's telling and re-telling. As Christians began to draw out the meaning of the life and work of Jesus for our human destiny they noted some passing references in the Old

Testament that seemed to have interpretative significance. In the prophet *Isaiah* (1:3) they found the chance statement, 'The ox knows his owner and the ass his master's crib' and in *Habbakuk* (3:2) they found the words, 'Between two beasts are you known.' In the light of their post-Easter conviction that the human Jesus was the incarnation of God, the earthly expression of the very being and presence with us of the divine Creator of the universe, whom even the ox and the ass know as their ultimate owner and master, it was easy to put two and two together. If Jesus was the one spoken of by the prophets, then at his birth his crib must be flanked by an ox and an ass. And so we have this today in the Christmas crib at the back of the cathedral, and as the focus of crib devotions in just about every church across the country and around the world throughout the Christmas season.

The three wise men were from an early time represented as kings, probably on the basis of a passing remark in *Psalm 72*, 'The kings of Tarshish and of the Isles render him tribute, may the kings of Sheba and Seba bring gifts!' In the sixth century they were assigned the names of Caspar, Melchior and Balthasar. By the Middle Ages one of them was usually depicted as white-skinned, European and middle-aged, one as a young black man, and the third as Asian, old and with a wispy grey beard. And this is the way the wise men are usually depicted to this day. All this is legendary, but it expresses a timely reminder of the Gospel truth that Christ has a multicultural significance. The representation of the wise men as kings of different skin pigment certainly signals the truth that Christ came to call together not just the like-minded and those of like ethnic origin, but to gather into one all things earthly and heavenly, including the young, the middle-aged and the old, in one intergenerational family.

In other words, Christmas has something important to say to us, not just about families and friends, not just about the local but about the global. At Christmas we bring before our mind's eye an image of the world hanging in space, like a great marbled blue and white iridescent Christmas decoration. All the world's inhabitants, regardless of their place of origin, are the children of God. Whatever our genetic and cultural inheritance, we are intended to live together as members of the human family in mutual respect, love and peace. That is the kind of community that Christ came to inaugurate by his radical transformation of Judaism to include the gentiles, the foreigners; this is the kind of community into which Christ continues to gather us.

These days we hear a good deal about multiculturalism in Australia, but our experience has made us painfully aware that the ideal of a multicultural Australia is fairly shallowly rooted. One suspects that it often goes little deeper than an unreflective appreciation of culinary variety in our restaurants, a consciousness of wontons and ravioli. Underneath a latent and potentially ugly racial intolerance seems to be lurking as a sinister threat to our social stability.

And this raises questions about the real basis of the Australian ideal of multiculturalism. Australians used to talk about the ideal of 'mateship' but that particular concept today sounds a bit old-fashioned – talk of being good mates does not seem to have much of a future in a world of gender equality. What in this generation do we have to put in its place? What kind of outcome do we really have in mind when we talk of multiculturalism, and where exactly do we get the ideal from? There must surely be more to it than wontons and ravioli.

Even without a clear ideology, a prudent wisdom might suggest that it is, pragmatically speaking, not wise to create enemies for yourself unnecessarily. Pauline Hanson was probably not inclined to take much notice of the Jewish Wisdom literature in the Old Testament, less likely to draw upon ancient Chinese wisdom. Were she more open to it she might well have noted the adage, 'She who treats a whole race of people with disdain is likely to be treated with disdain herself.' To some degree we create our own enemies. Indeed, it may take years, even decades, before the damage done in recent years to Australia's relations with our South East Asian neighbours is healed. Soured memories are long lasting, and we know that they can be tragically divisive and intractable as in Northern Ireland and between Serbs and Muslims in Bosnia.

Without a clearly articulated and shared set of national ideals we easy-going Australians tend to take a more evolutionary, hit and miss approach to social outcomes. On the basis of the principle of the survival of the fittest we tend to allow competing forces in society to jostle for place and hope for the best. Inevitably, the Australian ideological vacuum is filled by sectional interests and competing forces – economists, environmentalists, unionists, feminists, parliamentary lobbyists, pro- and anti-abortionists, monarchists and republicans, not to mention the economic rationalists. These tend to be more commonly referred to now as economic fundamentalists for there does not appear to be too much rationalism in the obsessive drive to achieve a quick bottom line balancing of the budget regardless of the social outcomes. All these competing forces vie for ascendancy while our parliaments, meanwhile, have the difficult task of seeking to provide the legislative constraints and sanctions necessary to hold it all together in some kind of unity. The outcome is that we edge uncertainly towards an unknown and ill-defined future, lurching from awkward compromise to awkward compromise. Certainly, the

Australian consciousness has nothing like the 'American dream', an ultimate vision of individual equality and equality of opportunity, to guide our path into the future, though we might not necessarily want to repeat the aggressive and, some would say, excessive individualism of the American experience.

We cross our fingers and hope for the best and perhaps are justified in the feeling that the end result will be determined, not by the merit of a case – a careful and corporately shared consensus about what is most desirable, good and life-giving – but simply by the sectional agenda of the ones who happen to shout the loudest.

So where do we get a clearer vision of a multicultural Australia from? Well, there may be no better source than the Gospel of Christ, with his radical call to love of neighbour and his insistent challenge to us to live with others in mutual respect, a call grounded in the conviction that there is one God and Creator of us all, and that God intends us to live together in a mutually enriching and diverse community of love and peace. There *must* be more to multiculturalism than wontons and ravioli.

In the celebration of Christmas we do not just look back to the past. The festival of the birth of Christ not only celebrates the one who first brought the possibility of redemption and renewal in love and peace to our human consciousness but also the arrival of the future, the dawning possibility of a world of love and peace, which the darker side of the human condition can never overcome. This is where we find the clearest vision for a multicultural Australia – indeed, for a multicultural world.

The Christian Church understands itself as that part of the world where the kingdom of God is already dawning; where, for all their imperfections, people hear its call and respond by aligning themselves with its good purposes and values. Our hearts are made glad by the yearly celebration of the incarnation of the Son of God because in our families at this time we glimpse the concrete experience of love and peace and of humanity generously disposed, redeemed and at one, which is the down payment and promise of the redemption of all men, women and children of every race and nation. If only all the world could experience what we at this time cherish and celebrate. In our Christmas celebration in our families, and in the goodwill of our local communities, we are conscious of being that part of the world where the future of God is arriving, where the values of the kingdom are already making an appearance. Our prayer is that we may play our part to light up the whole global sky with the light of peace, social harmony and human goodwill so that all the world may know the salvation of God.

22

CORNERED

PREACHED IN ST GEORGE'S CATHEDRAL, PERTH ON THE EVE OF
NATIONAL BREAST CANCER DAY, 26 OCTOBER 1997.

> Little Jack Horner
> Sat in the corner,
> Eating his Christmas pie.
> He put in his thumb
> And pulled out a plum,
> And said, 'What a good boy am I.'

It was not until I began to think about this sermon, at this service to mark national Breast Cancer Day, that I noticed the very wide range of uses to which we humans put the word 'corner'. Some of them carry overtones of comfort, satisfaction and enjoyment. In other words, a corner is often a good place to be in. Like little Jack Horner we are sometimes glad to be in our particular and familiar corner, away from the pressures and demands that others put upon us, just to enjoy our own piece of pie. And a corner is often a comfortable place to be in even if it is not a particularly big and expansive place – 'you in your small corner and me in mine'. Indeed, it is precisely because it is protected and snug that we 'curl up', as we say, 'in a corner with a book'.

Some of us have discovered quiet, relatively undisturbed and spiritually refreshing places which appeal to us as 'remote corners of the earth'; indeed, this south-west corner of the state of Western Australia is valued by those of us privileged to live here as a relatively undiscovered and precious jewel.

Sometimes we speak of glimpsing things out of 'the corner of our eye'. This cathedral was once served by a priest who suffered from the disadvantage of having no peripheral vision. He could only see what was immediately and directly in front of him. And the curious thing was that he grew up quite unaware of this physical disability.

His lack of peripheral vision was only discovered when he was tested for his driver's licence, on a memorable occasion when he reduced the licencing inspector to a trembling wreck by driving at speed through intersections apparently without so much as noticing what was approaching to the right and left. Needless to say he does not hold a driver's licence. Later, upon reflection, he came to realise that he had grown up thinking that tennis was a game in which you had to guess where the ball went when it disappeared from view. By contrast, most of us, fortunately, are very acutely sensitive to the slightest movement which we detect out of 'the corner of our eye'.

Then there are those corners that we can easily identify as meeting places or which we rely upon physically as we seek to find our way around. It is the street corner where we notice the city office worker waiting for his sweetheart to finish work for the day so that they can go off together. Street corners can likewise be the more sinister sites for illicit meetings, drug dealing, and the nefarious operations of the underworld.

Then there are those corners which we would prefer not to be in, when we feel cornered by circumstances beyond our control and from which there appears to be no escape. When we feel trapped, the psychological corner in which we find ourselves may trigger a number of responses. When we are first backed into a corner, and there appears to be no escape, we may, like frightened animals, simply tremble inwardly in anxiety and fear. It is more likely, however, that this kind of circumstance will trigger a response of anger and rage. When trapped and cornered we tend to lash out, the immediate expression of the basic instinct to survive. Certainly when we feel helpless and cornered by life's unwelcome and unexpected blows the emotional response can be immediate and volatile. When that initial reaction subsides a little it may be replaced by an ultimate and soul-penetrating sense of devastation, suffering and remorse, the anguished wish that one's circumstances were other than they are.

Something of the devastation of being in that particular kind of corner and having to come to terms with apparently life-shattering prospects is poignantly expressed in a painting by Joy Hester, entitled 'Girl in a Corner'. Slumped at a table, with her head down, and the other hand over her head, the picture says it all. The painting was done in 1957; Joy Hester eventually lost her battle with cancer in 1960.

I would be surprised if there are any of us who have not had some kind of experience of being cornered, trapped by circumstances beyond our control, with the attendant suffering that such a predicament brings. Coming to terms with the anguished wish that one's circumstances were other than they are may disturb our souls more dreadfully and in the longer term be more unbearable than actual physical pain. Today, to a large extent, physical pain can be controlled. We are blessed to live in an age when the science of pain control has advanced to a high level of effectiveness and is still advancing. But the anguish of psychological suffering may be much more difficult to come to terms with and to deal with satisfactorily. The loss of a loved one may take years to get over if, indeed, we ever really get over it.

In a more general, less immediate sense, of course, we are all cornered in this world. As humans, simply by being human, we know that we are born, we live and we die, for we are all mortal and from that there is no escape. From a Christian point of view there is victory over death but no escape from it. But we prefer to put the thought of that ultimate cornering out of mind. Indeed, a friend of mine in San Francisco was once addressing a gathering on the spirituality of loss and grief and, at one point, asked those in the group to put up their hand if they were in a terminal condition. 'Would you believe, nobody put up their hand.' But the reality is, of course, that we are all in a terminal condition. None of us will live for ever, but most of us put the thought of our mortality out of mind. Others are plunged into circumstances that make them acutely conscious of the fragility of life and of the sense of being cornered by the imminent approach of death. We never quite know what awaits us around the corner of the future.

What is the response of the Christian in the face of this kind of cornering? The answer is simple for it is the answer to our human condition generally, brought to bear on particular circumstance. It can be summed up in three words – faith and hope and love. Let me say something in turn about each of them.

The Christian answer to the facing of life's tragic blows is that, in our ultimate sense of creaturely dependence and in the face of the mystery of why anything should be, we have no alternative but to fall back on our basic trust that the universe is for us and not ultimately against us, that it is on our side. And the entire universe is ultimately for us and not against us because our God has been revealed as one who is for us and not against us, for God has promised to be with us come what may.

Faith cannot be manufactured in an instant, like instant coffee. It is not just stirred into the cup of life so that we have it conveniently handy. It is important to have reflected regularly over time so that one's belief commitments are in place before one is put to the test. This is the only way to develop a trustful receptivity to life and an abiding sense that the universe is on our side as a raft of support when times get tough.

Then there is hope. Humans are incurably oriented towards the future. We prepare for it, plan for it, save for it. And when times get tough and hopes are dashed, we find ourselves mysteriously bouncing back and preparing for a new day. But there is a difference between expecting, hoping, and mere wishful thinking. The difference resides in the degree of evidence that warrants the attitude. We rightly expect that the sun will rise tomorrow for there is plenty of scientific, incontrovertible scientific evidence to ground the expectation. There is no debate about it.

But when the evidence is a little ambiguous, when we are dealing with spiritual rather than physical matters and there is room for interpretation and a degree of freedom that allows us to move across the spectrum from pessimism to optimism, the best we can do is hope. We cannot expect things to turn out thus, and so, but we may have good grounds for hoping that this will be the case. For the Christian, the ground of hope resides in the promise of God, the promise to be with us and on our side.

But mere wishful thinking is that human attitude that has no rational underpinning. When the evidence is insufficient to ground an expectation or a hope we engage in wishful thinking.

Fortunately, in relation to the treatment of breast cancer, our situation at present is one predominantly of hope. With the great advances in early detection and diagnosis and treatment much earlier than in a former age, the news is good.

There are certainly grounds for hope – genuine hope that is not just wishful thinking. This is why individuals privately, and governments corporately, can be encouraged to support breast cancer research programs. There are now very good grounds for believing, trusting and hoping that any money put into this area of medical endeavour will be very well spent.

Then there is love. Christian love is different from faith and hope in one very important respect. For while the faith is our faith, and the hope our hope, the love is God's love. 'The love of God has been poured into our hearts by the Holy Spirit who has been given to us' (*Romans* 5:5). The great love of God is revealed in his Son. This particular and unconditional love is available to us despite our unworthiness, our many apparent failures, our sheer human foolishness. The great love of God revealed in his Son is, in turn, revealed, though in less perfect, more fragmentary and less clearly focused ways in those who follow Christ and his way of love.

The great love of God that we know in Christ and in the lives of those who follow him is the one reason both for our faith and our hope. That love is the ground of our believing trust and the promise of more love to come, for which we hope. Once we understand the love of God revealed in his Son as the basis of our faith and hope, there is ultimately no cornering that can contain us.

We may, as we live our Christian lives, have to face the trauma of the prospect of untimely death; we may not escape the humanly shattering experience of the loss of a loved one. And for all of us there is no escape from death some day at some time, but there is always the victory born of faith and hope and grounded in the great love of God revealed in his Son. There may not be escape but in the battle with breast cancer there will be victory.

23

THE APPLE OF OUR REDEMPTION

PREACHED IN ST GEORGE'S CATHEDRAL, PERTH
ON CHRISTMAS DAY, 25 DECEMBER 1997.

As I drove into the city of Perth across the causeway from south of the river, I noticed green and red flags greeting me. I had trouble discerning what they were meant to signal for there was no wind and they hung limp so it was difficult to see the emblem on them. Eventually I noticed that one flag carried the city arms and the words 'City of Perth', and others bore a star, a Christmas tree and a somewhat stylised reindeer.

It should have occurred to me that these were Christmas flags without having to see their emblems, for the combination of red and green speaks clearly enough of Christmas. Some people in some parts of the world may dream of a white Christmas, but all the world over red and green have become the predominant colours at this time of the year. Why is this so?

One reason is, of course, that we have assimilated this part of the culture of Christmas from the celebration's European origins. In the deep mid-winter there are no flowers. Decoration, particularly in churches, necessarily relies on Christmas greenery, holly and ivy, with a touch of red from the holly berries. But there is a little more to the red and green of Christmas than that.

In order to grasp the meaning behind the colours we have to go back about a thousand years. By the Middle Ages it had become fashionable to decorate churches at Christmas time, beside the altar or at either side of the Chancel arch, with Christmas trees. Upon them were hung shining red apples. In the course of time, the real apples were replaced by artificial ones which, in turn, became the coloured baubles with which we are all familiar.

Apples were hung originally on Christmas trees, not just for their red colour, but because of their deeply religious significance. Medieval Christians were perhaps more conscious than we are of the role of the apple in the primal symbolic act of human disobedience. As the fifteenth century carol says, 'Adam lay ybounden, bounden in a bond' – in other words the devil had got into him. And we know today our solidarity with Adam. We know the fundamental human tendency to imagine that we can somehow live successfully in this world independently of our Creator – to try to be even as God by going it alone, free and unfettered by the moral constraints of living in accordance with the divine intention and will for us. And we know the consequences, the red of blood and suffering. We know the fault.

But today we celebrate the remedy. For the coming of Christ on that first Christmas brought down the curtain on the faulty humanity of the old Adam and a new day dawned. And medieval Christians hung their bright red apples on their Christmas trees, in a sense to poke fun at the original apple of the fall, that rotten apple as it turned out, to signal the reversal of the human tendency of failure to fulfil the divine intention of our human potential. The brightly coloured apples on our Christmas trees, even those that today are often so stylised, celebrate the perpetual possibility of our human renewal and redemption in Christ. These are the sweet new apples of our redemption.

Indeed, for one strain of ancient Christian thought, Adam's fault did not involve a fall from an original state of perfect obedience. Rather, Adam's fault was a failure to rise to the standard God set and intended, a failure to move on to a higher plane of moral and spiritual well-being. God did not suddenly realise that he must switch to plan B and send his Son to correct an original fault that he had inadvertently left in Creation by giving Adam and Eve the freedom to do their own thing and so to get themselves in a mess. It was always part of the divine plan from all eternity to send the Son to lift his creatures on to a new plane of existence in harmony and peace. The birth of the new Adam heralded the next phase of spiritual and moral growth and development. And this means that Adam's original taking of the apple was not all bad. As the carol once again puts it, in a curious sentence with the verb at the end that probably betrays an original translation from German, 'Blessed be the time that apple taken was; Therefore, we must singen *Deo gracias*' – thanks be to God for the apple, for the apple Adam took, for had that not happened, had humans not been in need of perfection, Christ would not have come and we would not now be celebrating all the joyous possibilities of the new humanity.

Some have lamented the absence of symbols in the city expressing the 'true meaning of Christmas' but, perhaps unwittingly, the true meaning of Christmas is everywhere around us. The strings of brightly coloured baubles hung, not only on Christmas trees, but also across the streets are all, whether those who put them there were conscious of the fact or not, really apples, the bright new apples of our redemption. Christmas is for everybody, everybody who may pass under those brightly coloured apples: children and families, single people, rainbow coloured people, gay and lesbian people, the lonely and the unloved, the marginalised, the unemployed. Christmas is the celebration together of our human redemption, the making new of our humanity in shared well-being.

Curiously, in our culture, because we tend to lose our grasp of the true meaning of things, we tend to shuffle a sense of human renewal off until the celebration of New Year. This is traditionally the time for making fresh resolutions about how we shall be and what we shall do in the year ahead. Both for us as individuals and as a community it provides the opportunity to start life afresh.

We are realistic enough to know, of course, that in all probability we will very quickly break our New Year resolutions. That is, after all, a natural part of our humanity. We know the fault. But we nevertheless feel the pressure of each New Year to review where we have been and what we have so far made of ourselves so as to make some kind of a new start.

So we may resolve this coming year to stop smoking, or to manage work demands and spend more time with our families. We may resolve to manage our finances better or make sure that this year we get our tax return in on time. We target all those things where we missed the mark last time round. As a community, no less than as individuals however, we know deep down that things are going to be much the same. We know the fault. The same old troubles will be with us. It could be unemployment, house break-ins and theft, drug-taking, suicide, low morale and continuing public niggling about possible corruption in the police force. The same unresolved debates will continue – the legalisation against living off the earnings of a prostitute, euthanasia, pokie machines in pubs, global warming and the degradation of the environment. An adequate acknowledgement of the mistreatment of the stolen generation of Aboriginal children will inevitably continue to irritate, for it seems that the opportunity of an apology is unfortunately lost. A forced, begrudging apology, wrung from a government under public duress, would hardly be a genuine apology at all. Wik and the rights and wrongs of Native Title, and co-existence in a diverse and inclusive Australia will still be around to challenge our inherent human tendency to think in terms of our own racial superiority. All these issues will continue to distract, disturb and divide us. There is nothing much here that is new. We know the fault.

Perhaps what we need to do is to consider and make our own the message of Christmas before New Year – the message not just about the fault but about the remedy. We need to look again at what Christ has done for us in the renewal of our humanity, by breaking down the barrier erected by Adam's disobedience, freeing us from the bond with which 'Adam was ybounden' and calling us on to the life of love and obedient discipleship under God.

Hearing the call of the New Adam, we may all resolve to set aside those sinister tendencies that move within us, those humanly restricting and deforming tendencies of the old Adam that we all know – to be ungenerous, mealy mouthed, prejudiced, self-concerned and self-interested – and to bring a fresh spirit to the assessment of all those old public issues that we can be sure will continue to hassle us. It may be that, even if we break the resolve from time to time, the net benefit to us and our society of that kind of resolution will be far greater than we imagine. We know the remedy. And that is why we dare to celebrate together as families, as single people and as a community, the new apple of our redemption.

Deo gracias! Thanks be to God!

24

ANNUNCIATION

PREACHED ON THE OCCASION OF THE CELEBRATION OF THE
CENTENARY OF THE MOTHERS' UNION IN WESTERN AUSTRALIA,
IN ST GEORGE'S CATHEDRAL, PERTH ON THE FEAST OF THE
ANNUNCIATION OF THE BLESSED VIRGIN MARY, 25 MARCH 1998.

B elieve it or not, it is only 276 days till Christmas! A quick count from this annual celebration of the angel's announcement to the Blessed Virgin Mary on the 25 March to the celebration of Christ's birth on 25 December is exactly nine months and this, if I have computed it accurately, is 276 days – the exact period from conception to birth at full term.

I suppose, as we bring the scene of the annunciation of the angel to Mary before our mind's eye, it will inevitably be informed by one or other of the many representations of the episode from the great tradition of Christian art – perhaps with the angel on one knee, bedecked with an impressive plumage and with a very demure, perhaps even bemused, Virgin. In one image that comes to my mind, a dove also hovers in the window, suggestive of the Holy Spirit, and a fine shaft of light crosses the room to penetrate the Virgin's ear. In the Middle Ages it was understood that the conception of the Christ child was effected through the Virgin's ear. It was, after all, something wrought by command of the Word of God, miraculously and instantaneously, just as God spoke and *all things* came to be.

In any event, whatever concrete image the story of the angel announcing the good news to Mary brings to your mind's eye, the effect of the announcement in *our ears* is to bring Bethlehem forwards into the present in a totally premature and intrusive way, that even outdoes the attempts of retailers in October or November to coax us to turn our minds to Bethlehem long before it seems appropriate. And today's announcement of 'only 276 days till Christmas' is all the more a jolt to us because we are smack in the middle of Lent. Our hearts and minds, as involved and committed Christian people, are focused at this time of the year on the death and resurrection of Jesus. We naturally find it a disturbance in the lead-time to Calvary and Easter to have our minds forcibly turned to Bethlehem by the announcement of Christ's birth.

The intrusion of Bethlehem into the time of the more sober themes of Christ's passion and death is a reminder to us, however, that we must always, at all times, be alert and ready for Christ's coming into the world – even when our world seems reflective and subdued or seriously preoccupied with its shadow side or even very pessimistic and hopelessly gloomy. It is rather pointless for us to focus on the first century story of the annunciation of the angel to Mary, in whatever concrete image that may come to mind, unless we hear that annunciation news as the ever-present possibility of the coming to birth of Christ in us. For as we who have ears to hear respond to the Word of God to us, he comes to birth in us.

There is a sense in which everything that happened to Christ during his lifetime on earth happens over and over, in a kind of eternal recapitulation. What happened to Christ happens to us, for the events of Christ's life are the events of our human pilgrimage. Indeed, one way of understanding the spiritual life of the Christian is to see that, in some way, everything that happened to Christ has to happen to us – his birth in us as well as his death and resurrection in us – for a disciple is not above his master. One of the early Church Fathers, Gregory of Nazianzus wrote, 'We have to bear everything that Christ bore – the birth, the nails and the resurrection.'

In the contemporary world it is apparently not difficult to interpret the stirring of spiritual renewal in human hearts in terms of 'being born again', especially in the United States where they not only experience it in a very focused and clear kind of way, but also talk openly and at great length about it. But even if talking about it does not come so easily to us, it happens to us, and it happens again and again. Likewise we have experiences of suffering and difficulty and then of overcoming these – dying and rising to new life. Our experiences of disappointment, depression and suffering, trauma, grief, rescue from the brink of disaster, and then of love and reawakening to life and joy, have something of death and resurrection about them. But that experience of death and resurrection is the very experience that can be interpreted also in terms of the pain of travail and of birth with the attendant joy that a child has been born into the world. In other words, Calvary and Easter on one hand and Bethlehem on the other are somehow about the same kind of thing. The birth of Christ's Spirit in us and the paschal renewal of Christ in us at Easter are the same kind of experience.

So the announcement of Bethlehem in Lent is not as out of place as it may at first seem. We can if we look hard enough point to experiences in our own lives, however trivial they may seem, which can be interpreted as our Bethlehem ... or as our Calvary and Easter. As Christ himself comes to birth in us, our thoughts and words and deeds become pregnant with his Spirit. To use an Easter symbol: the new life of Christ's love flickers to life in us to make us generously open to others when formerly we were spiritually dead – tightly wound and sealed in the grave of our own self-concern.

Another way of saying this is that, as the thin shaft of light of the address of God penetrates our inner ear and we respond in faith and obedient discipleship, the image of God comes to birth in us. And when our lives are pregnant with the image of God we are most authentically human. A Jewish Rabbi in the Middle Ages once said that every human being is preceded by a legion of angels crying, 'Make way for the image of God! Make way for the image of God!'

Think of what that angelic annunciation might mean for the way we treat one another. When we appreciate that the image of God is coming to birth in us we can take a look at our neighbour, or at the person next to us at work (just a quick, sidelong glance that he or she will not notice) and, if we have an eye to see, we see there a Bethlehem – a dwelling place for the coming to birth of the image of God too. When we become aware of that possibility we hear again the story of the angel's announcement as a message or call to us to help bring the image of God to birth in the world. Indeed, just as Christ came to physical birth from the womb of his mother Mary, so the Spirit of Christ is to come to birth not just in us but in the world through and from us.

This means that we are all, in a sense, midwives, insofar as we are all helpers in the task of bringing to birth the image of

God in others. That, of course, has been the traditional vocation of the Mothers' Union whose centenary in Western Australia we are also celebrating today. For one hundred years members of the Mothers' Union have heard the call to uphold the family, to be faithful wives and mothers, to care for children ... yes, all these things. But in addition, and in relation to all members of all families, both husbands and children and the extended family of Christ in neighbourly community, members of the Mothers' Union have heard the call to be midwives to the birth of Christ, so as to assist in the delivery of God in and to the world. For the Mothers' Union also, as for every institution that is truly alive, there will be experiences of dying and rising again.

The story of Bethlehem reminds us that Christ can come to birth even in the most unpromising, broken-down and unexpected of circumstances. God is not too fussy. He has no delicate taste for his love knows no bounds. This means that he accepts us as we are, if we only make a little room for him. There can be no room for him, of course, if we are 'full of ourselves'.

But if he comes to us as we humbly are, just as he has promised, he also comes to our world *as it is*, to situations that, on the face of it, are not too promising – collapsed peace talks, the stresses and strains created by failing economies, the break-down of health systems. He comes to the shambles we humans collectively make of the world – socially, politically, morally and environmentally. In it all he comes to birth. And we are to be midwife to him.

We know that from our quiet obedience great things result, just as from the quiet obedience of Mary, brought to term in a stable, came the salvation of the world. If God can use such unlikely material as that of the first Bethlehem, he can surely use the likes of us. The only difference is that between the moment of the angel's announcement to us today and the future coming to birth of the image of God in us and among those with whom we have to do, we do not have to wait 276 days. The thin shaft of light of the Word of God enters our ear, we open ourselves to the birth of Christ in us and in others through us, and it happens here ... and it happens now ... miraculously and instantaneously. Thanks be to God.

25

WALKING ON WAVES

PREACHED ON 14 MARCH 1999 AT THE CELEBRATION
OF THE SIXTIETH ANNIVERSARY OF THE PARISH OF ST PATRICK,
MT LAWLEY, PERTH ON THE GOSPEL FOR THE DAY:
MATTHEW 14: 22–33.

The story of Jesus walking on the water is one which inevitably raises a number of questions including the unavoidable and basic question: Did it really happen? Did Jesus really walk on water? Did he really command Peter to do the same thing? And did Peter also actually walk on water until his attention was diverted by the stormy wind? Did Peter sink only because of his lack of faith?

That certainly is the suggestion in the story for, as Peter began to be afraid and to sink, he called out to Jesus, 'Save me Lord!' At once, we are told, Jesus grabbed him and said, 'How little faith you have. Why did you doubt?' The implication seems to be that with sufficient faith we could walk on water. But is that what the story is intended to teach?

A biblical fundamentalist would certainly urge us to read that story as a literal description of what happened. His or her basic presupposition is that the Bible is absolutely, unchangeably and self-evidently true in a purely factual sense. No interpretation is needed because scripture is assumed to be a body of literal and factual information. This is roughly what the Muslim fundamentalist also believes about the Koran. For the Christian fundamentalist there is no question about it. Scripture says that Jesus walked on water, Peter walked on water, and Peter only sank because of his lack of faith — and what the Bible says is infallibly true. The Bible is treated as a 'paper pope', a source of literal and infallible truths. It does not raise questions or challenge us so much as state answers in such a way that our questions and doubts are made to appear sub-Christian and wrong.

Nevertheless, most of us will still be troubled, if we are prepared to be honest with ourselves, by the questions raised. Did it really happen? And how are we to answer?

Some have attempted to justify the belief that the walking on water happened in the manner in which it is reported by eliminating or reducing the apparently miraculous and supernatural aspect of it — Jesus was actually walking ankle deep on a sandbank. What happened when Peter jumped out of the boat was that he was lucky enough to strike a sandbank too. You know how quickly water depth can change. One minute you can be up to your ankles or knees and the next up to your waist and neck. So the walking on the water and the Peter's sudden fear and sinking and being rescued by Jesus is explained naturalistically in an attempt to retain a purely literal and descriptive reading of what happened.

Some accounts of the feeding of the five thousand follow a similar approach suggesting that when the little boy generously produced his five barley loaves and two small fishes and offered to share them, he shamed all the crowd into producing their sandwiches and picnic hampers from under their cloaks in order to share with those who had nothing. The story of a literal feeding of five thousand is thus handled by explaining away its miraculous side. Likewise, a literal reading of the walking on the water can be defended by appeal to a sandbank.

After 2000 years there is no way we can make up the deficiency of the fragmentary evidence we have in the Bible to resolve the question either way. Whether there was a sandbank there or not is an open question.

Those of us who are less committed to a nervous defence of a literal or surface reading of the story may be open to the suggestion, however, that the story as we have it is one that has undergone some development in the course of its transmission. In the sixty-year period between the death of Jesus and when Matthew wrote (possibly about AD 90) the story has been passed around orally, drafted and redrafted, told and retold. In a sense it has grown by being added to in the telling.

It is also possible that in this process of oral transmission it got misplaced in the sequence of events. It is possible, for example, that while this incident is presented by Matthew as one which occurred during Jesus' lifetime, prior to his crucifixion, it was originally an Easter narrative. The one who came to the fishermen disciples, over the water as it were, so that they became aware of his presence with them in the boat and thus fell down in worship calling him 'Son of God', was the Easter Jesus. He came to them just as he comes to us across the centuries to be present in our eucharist or when two or three are gathered in his name. He comes to us just as he has come to hundreds of others over the sixty-year history of this parish Church.

It was thus originally not so much a physical walking across the waters as an appearance of the heavenly and exalted Jesus. Some have said also that the Easter narrative which constituted the original kernel of the story was perhaps the account of Jesus' first appearance to Peter, which is not depicted anywhere else in the New Testament. Paul says that Jesus appeared to Peter and the twelve, singling out Peter by name, and Luke concludes the story of the Easter appearance on the road to Emmaus by having the disciples return to Jerusalem where they find others declaring 'that Jesus is risen indeed and has appeared to Peter', but we have no actual description of an appearance to Peter.

Thus it can be argued that what is declared in these traditions is actually described in a story of Jesus meeting with Peter at the lakeside, which provides the original kernel of the story that later got filled out and misplaced in Jesus' earlier lifetime as the 'walking on the water' story.

That an Easter narrative provided the original background of this story is suggested also by the account of the Easter appearance to the seven in John's Gospel. In *John* 21 Jesus appears on the shore and Peter leaps into the water to go to him, wading towards him through (not upon) the water. Has this Easter story in *John* been transformed by *Matthew* and placed by mistake as an episode in the earthly life of Jesus prior to his crucifixion?

Once again at 2000 years remove we have insufficient evidence to resolve the historical issue. What we can say, loud and clear, is that different interpretations of this story are certainly possible, and we should be wary of biblical fundamentalists who insist that their literal and purely factual reading of the story is the only legitimate reading of it. For while they argue that scripture is literally true and needs no interpretation, a literal or surface reading of it is very much their interpretation, which they insist on forcing upon everybody. There are certainly other possibilities.

Those of us, for example, who are committed, not so much to the literal truth of the Bible, but to a belief and trust in the living presence of our Lord Jesus Christ, faith is a personal relationship rather than a kind of assent to the truth of a set of literal propositions. When we turn from the person of Jesus to the Bible as the record of what the first Christians said about their relationship with Jesus, as they struggled to express in words what that faith meant to them, we are freed to hear the story in a different way. Given the centrality for us of the living Christ himself, we may be less wedded to a defence of the literal historical truth of the episode of the 'walking on the water' and more interested in interpreting the meaning of the story for us and for our life of faith today.

We may see less truth of a literal kind and more of a symbolic kind. We know, for example, that from the earliest days the image of a ship was used by the first believers to signify the Church. Just as Noah and his family were rescued from the rising flood in a great ark or ship, so in the rising flood of the insecure and storm-tossed secular world people are saved by God as he calls them to himself and into the community of faith — the Christian Church. The Church is the ark of salvation in the modern world, sailing ahead towards the safe haven of human tranquillity, reconciliation, love and peace.

We are very conscious today of what may await us in the future. Given the perilous nature of our world — with its wars and its weapons, its social instability and moral upheaval, its frighteningly aggressive nationalism, its marriage breakdown and racial insult, its anguish and tears — we cry out 'Save us Lord!' We call for help lest we get swamped and sink and are lost in the rising flood of the stormy world in which we live. It is over the storm-tossed waters of this world that our Lord comes to us. And it is in the ship of the Church that we, having heard the call to Christian discipleship, realise what little faith we have. But it is precisely in this fearfulness that we recognise the power of Christ alone to seize hold of us and rescue us and ultimately calm the storm. It is within the ship of the Church that we fall down in worship and confess our faith that truly Jesus is the Son of God. It is not for nothing that the body of the Church is called a nave and the pulpit its poop deck from which the lieutenants of the Captain shout directions and words of encouragement to the sailors.

The story of the walking on the water may be not so much a literal statement of what happened in the remote past, but rather a story that expresses truths about us and our experience in the ship of the Church, whose fellowship becomes for us the ark of salvation. If we read this Gospel story with an ear to hear it is a story about us, we will find that it is unquestionably true, for we find it to be true in our experience.

Today we celebrate sixty years of the life of this ark in which countless people have found salvation. And today we pray for Christ to be present with us as we point the bow into the winds of the unknown future of this troubled and stormy world.

26

ORDINATION VOWS

PREACHED TO THE GATHERED CLERGY OF THE DIOCESE OF PERTH
AT THE ANNUAL CHRISM EUCHARIST IN ST GEORGE'S CATHEDRAL,
PERTH ON MAUNDY THURSDAY, 1 APRIL 1999.

At this eucharist, apart from gathering together for the breaking of the bread and the sharing of the cup, and the prayers, we are here to do three additional things.

First, as part of our preparation for the Easter ceremonies of the next three days we consecrate the oil of Chrism. This oil will be used on Easter morning and throughout the coming year in the context of Christian initiation by baptism into the death and resurrection of Christ with water, and the laying on of a hand with prayer for the strengthening gift of the Spirit. Today we consecrate the oil that will be for us in the coming year, as it were, an evangelical tool of trade.

In addition to the consecration of the oil of Chrism, we also take the opportunity to consecrate the oil of the sick, for use with prayer and the laying on of hands, in the Church's ministry of healing. Once again, the oil of the sick provides us with another of our tools of trade for the coming year.

Finally there is the renewal of ordination vows, which comes to focus on yet another laying on of hands, though not in the Anglican tradition, accompanied by anointing. It is about this third item that I wish to speak today.

The renewal of our ordination vows takes place in the context of a discussion which, ironically, tends to undermine the very necessity of ordination to priesthood. If you open up the web page of the Diocese of Sydney, you will find the confident declaration that this is the age of the ministry of the laity, the ministry of those not ordained. This assertion is a prelude to an array of posted papers relating to the contention that deacons and lay people might well be licenced to preside at the eucharist. It is as though, having given some the gift of ordination, the Church might now blur the differentiation of roles between ordained and unordained people by extending some of the key functions to lay people that were formerly assigned uniquely to priests.

Perhaps we have unwittingly contributed both in our talk and in our behaviour to the dilution in public consciousness of the uniqueness of the role of the ordained. We are more than glad to affirm that this is the age of the re-discovery, through the identification of gifts, of the ministry of the laity. As St Paul would say: To each baptised person his or her own gift; and each is obliged to use his or her gift 'for the common good' as a contribution to the building up of the body of Christ. Over the last generation talk of the Church 'not as a community gathered around a minister' but as itself 'a ministering community' minimises the importance of the role of the ordained person.

There is a widespread tendency to minimise distinctions between clergy and laity in a variety of subtle ways. Even the tendency of clergy to abandon distinctive clerical dress, which is sometimes of concern to lay people at the Perth Diocesan synod, appears to be driven by the quest to identify with people generally; to be an ordinary sort of bloke or a regular kind of girl. The motives in terms of the facilitation of communication are undoubtedly well intentioned and good. Nevertheless this minimises the differences in roles.

Talk of the Church not being a community gathered around an ordained minister so much as a ministering community itself, leads automatically to the suggestion that the Church as a whole throws up people for leadership roles who are eventually authorised by ordination to perform certain functions. This would mean that the Church thus designates some to minister within its life as ordained priests and deacons. Ministry, in this manner of thinking, is the outcome of the Church's decision to organise and delegate. This is something of an illusion.

The bishop, when he ordains a lay person to the diaconate may be understood to act as leader and representative of the Church at large, but he also ordains as one who has himself been ordained deacon. The bishop ordains against the background authority of Christ the deacon who, in the foot-washing, so graphically demonstrated that he came not to be served but to serve, and he ordains as himself servant of the servants of the people of God. Ordination is not just an act of the Church through the bishop but also and always the act of a predecessor in the same office.

This dynamic is even clearer in the case of the consecration of bishops, given the requirement that the ministers of the ordination and consecration of a bishop must be at least three in number who have themselves already been consecrated bishop. A bishop, in other words, is consecrated by his or her predecessors in the office. And when it comes to the ordination of priests, it is not the Church at large that does the ordaining. Rather, all priests present with the presiding bishop participate in the laying on of hands. Ordination occurs at the hands of predecessors in office. That this has always been so is clear from the Epistles to Timothy where at one point hands are laid on presbyters by the assembled presbyters, and at another hands are laid on the originating authority of the apostle himself (*1 Timothy* 4: 14; *1 Timothy* 5:22; and *2 Timothy* 1:6).

It is true that the Church at large may have a role in the selection of candidates, and may formally consent to the ordination, but the actual setting apart, the authorising and empowering with the gift of the Spirit, is done by predecessors of the ordination candidates in the same office.

In other words, ordained ministry is not just something thrown up from within the Church by the Church. The Church does not by a kind of social contract delegate certain functions to specified persons within its own ranks. Rather, the ordained are set apart and differentiated *from* the Church at large, and this is given effect by the fact that they are ordained by their predecessors in office. This is part of what it means to be admitted to an order of ministers.

All of us who have been ordained have had hands laid upon us by our predecessors in the same office, so we enjoy participation in the historical continuity of a ministry that is marked by continuity of faith and practice though time, going back to the foundational ministry of the apostles. I guess this is what we have in mind when we speak of apostolic succession.

However, once again, we have tended to minimise the so-called 'pipeline' theory of apostolic succession that so much stressed the tactile connectedness of bishops, from bishop to bishop back to the original apostolic band. Instead, we have concentrated on the importance of the succession of the whole Church in apostolic faith and practice as the most important thing. This is ecumenically prudent and attractive to us because it provides common ground with those Churches which share with us a commitment to the faith of the apostles even if the historical continuity of their ministries has in some cases been fractured, perhaps for some at the time of the Reformation. Others have never had a pretence to historical continuity or original apostolic connection, as in the case of the contemporary bubble phenomenon of Churches founded and led by a self-appointed charismatic figure. In our tradition we have all been ordained by our predecessors in office, and this links us through time with the apostolic office.

The renewal of our ordination vows on this particular day reminds us that those to whom the gift of the eucharist was originally given and those who were originally mandated to 'do this' as a perpetual memorial of Christ's passion and death, were the very ones who on Easter Day were sent out as witnesses to his resurrection with a commission to take the Easter good news to the ends of the earth. If the apostles were in a sense the whole Church, the original community of faith, they were also and at the same time the original ministry, the original college of apostolic witnesses, sent out as ministers of sacrament and word in their mission to the world.

In a sense, the apostles were there before the Church was, for the Church is the community of those brought together by the speaking and hearing of the Gospel. The apostles were the first to utter it. A Church without an office of ministry has never existed; the one was originally coterminous with the other.

This means that right from the very start the life and mission of the Church was driven by ministry and not vice versa. It was certainly not that first there was the Church as one undifferentiated community of believers and then somebody thought up the bright idea of the differentiation of roles and orders of ministry. The ordained are not raised up from within the Church by the Church and then given certain specified tasks to perform on behalf of the Church by the Church at large. This is why the ordained minister is set apart by the laying on of hands, not by the Church at large, but by predecessors in the same office of ministry. Ordination with prayer and the laying on of hands arose as a necessity in the Church as a result of the absence of the apostles. Upon the death of the last apostle, the need for continuity of faith and for authentic witnesses to minister to the rest of the community became vitally important.

This also means that, in a sense, the gift of the eucharist was given to the Church but, at the same time, it was given to the Church's initiating apostolic office. We renew our ordination vows on Maundy Thursday because this is the day when the mandate to celebrate the eucharist was given in the assembly of the apostolic band, which is the basis of our continuing commission as those who stand in their succession. Today we receive anew the mandate of the eucharist as a most important evangelical tool of trade, as it were, in the on-going work of building community in the communion of God.

The foundational importance of the differentiation of roles and the primacy of ministry in the Church's mission is something to make our own as we renew our ordination vows today.

The fact that the ordinand receives ordination from predecessors in office means that those ordained retain not just a certain differentiation of role but also a functional distance *from* the Church at large. This is vitally important in the life of the Church for this is what enables the bishop, priest or deacon the freedom to minister not just in and on behalf of the Church, but also *to* the Church. We who are ordained are consecrated and set apart from the world and from the Church because we are called to speak, not just what the Church at large may want to hear, but prophetically to the Church, to be really authentic ministers of the Word *of God.* Our task is to deliver more than a message from the Church; the Word of God must be on our lips. Ordination sets us apart and frees us *from* the Church in order that we may fulfil this role. Setting apart or differentiation of function within the Church, which ordination by the laying on of hands by predecessors in office signals, in a sense allows the ordained minister to stand at a functional distance from the rest of the Church. It means he or she can address it authoritatively with the Word of God with a freedom *from* the community *for* the benefit of the community and the purity of the Gospel.

But the exercise of this ministerial freedom from the Church so as to minister to the Church, proves its authenticity only by unanimity and historical continuity of its message with the teaching of the apostles. Hence the promise to teach as necessary to salvation only what is 'contained in' the apostolic scriptures 'or may be proved thereby'. And once again, a sense of the importance of this authenticating continuity with the faith of the apostles is sealed by the same sign of continuity constituted by the laying on of hands by predecessors in the same office.

This is the age of lay ministry, and it is right to speak of the Church as a ministering community, but *at the same time* it is a community marked from the outset by the differentiation of roles, a community called together by the ministry of the Gospel and thus gathered around an ordained minister. Those of us who have had hands laid upon us by our predecessors in office and who today renew our lifelong vow and promise with prayer for the stirring up of the free gift of the Spirit that is within us, do well to ponder these awesome things.

27

JUSTIFICATION

PREACHED AT ST GEORGE'S CATHEDRAL, PERTH
ON EASTER DAY, 23 APRIL 2000.

ROMANS 4:25: CHRIST WAS HANDED OVER FOR OUR OFFENCES,
AND RAISED FOR OUR JUSTIFICATION.

Those of us who work on a computer or with a word processor will be familiar with an array of time-saving procedures, some of which also save us from embarrassment such as the spell check, and others that save us from messy presentation of written work by the neat formatting of documents. One of these is a simple procedure for justifying the margins of a text.

When a text is justified, the uneven and ragged line endings are all instantaneously lined up so that the margin is made neat and even. The justification of the text happens in a moment. As soon as you click on the appropriate formatting icon, the edges of the text are all miraculously straightened out.

I wonder how many contemporary computer wizzes are aware, however, that the term 'justification' is also essentially a biblical and theological term. Its meaning, when used in a religious context, bears a family resemblance with its meaning in relation to straightening up the margins of the text on the computer screen. When St Paul says *we* are justified by faith not by works, he means that when we open our hearts to God, when we click on God as it were, we are put right, instantaneously straightened up in his eyes so that we are enabled to walk straight and upright and with confidence before him.

The 'straightening out' language associated with justification is not unlike the less religious but moral language used when one parent says to another that it is time to sit down and give a good talking to a wayward teenager so as to 'straighten her out', or when a reformed criminal assures us that he is now 'going straight'. But the vital difference between the moral and our more clearly religious language is that we do not justify or straighten ourselves out by simply determining to do better. Salvation in the Christian understanding of things is not a reward or a tick for going straight and doing well. It is the freely offered forgiveness and acceptance of God even when we fail to do well. Justification has to do with God's initiative in sorting out the frayed and jumbled ends of life for us to give us a fresh start and set us on the right track.

So, our Christian conviction is that we are saved from the mess we tend to make of the text of our lives, when in faith and trust we click on God. And this happens by grace alone.

One of the great debates of the Reformation hinged on whether St Paul's use of the term 'justification' meant that God *declared* us righteous, or *accounted* us just and straight in his eyes, while we remained deep down essentially sinners, or whether he actually *made* us righteous by the infusion of grace, effecting a real change in us *actually* to straighten us out.

For Lutherans, Roman Catholic talk of the need of sanctification as part of our justification or straightening out before God suggested a need for human good works. However, they wanted to underline the truth that the whole thing was the unmerited gift of God. Roman Catholics thought that Lutheran talk of justification in terms only of God 'accounting us righteous', as though it simply involved a change in his attitude to us, forgiving us while we remained essentially sinful, was somehow inadequate. Sanctification was surely needed, they said, to effect a change in us and make us holy.

In the Reformation debates there seems also to have been a hidden difference in relation to time. For the Lutherans, God's accounting of us as righteous was momentary, something appropriated from the timeless eternity of God. It was a benefit that could be made one's own instantaneously by faith alone. From the Roman Catholic perspective a believer could be made righteous, good and holy only over time. It involved a process rather than a point in time.

As in many of the theological disputes of the past we can now see that they were really saying the same thing, but mishearing each other. In the heat of debate they misrepresented each other and worked with false stereotypes of what they thought the other's position to be. During this last year Lutherans and Roman Catholics have joyously celebrated the publication of an Agreed Statement on Justification in which they affirm that they together see justification as God's free and saving action in Christ, whereby our sin is forgiven and we are both *declared and made* righteous. In other words, we are accounted righteous by God instantaneously simply through faith in him, but the free acceptance of his divine forgiving self-communication is the mechanism through which we are then sanctified, actually straightened out and set upon the straight and narrow path that leads to life. The relationship with God established by grace though faith and trust in him changes us and redirects the way we live our lives and we actually become a new creation in Christ.

Certainly we rejoice that, after 450 years of fractured relationship triggered by differences of opinion on this particular doctrine, Lutherans and Roman Catholics have reached an ecumenical consensus. But I am drawing your attention to this straightening-out process called justification also because there is a clear connection between justification and Easter. 'Christ died for our offences and was raised for our justification' (*Romans* 4:25). Christ was handed over as 'a full, perfect and sufficient sacrifice, and satisfaction for the sins of the whole world', and was raised up in the interests of setting us straight.

But if Christ was raised for our justification, raised so as to straighten us out, just how did his resurrection do that? Indeed, how does his resurrection come into it at all?

Well, it is through trusting faith in God and our commitment to live faithful lives of obedient discipleship that we open ourselves to the free play of the Spirit of God. And it is through the in-dwelling gift of the Spirit that we are caught up into a living relationship with Him (*Romans* 8:14–17). Insofar as we are partakers of the divine nature we are sanctified; we become holy by grace alone. The Easter experience of Christians is not just that we are given new life by the ventilating presence of the Spirit of God, but that the Spirit in our experience bears the mark, the identifiably distinctive, remembered character of Jesus Christ himself. Thus, in the famous resurrection discourse in *I Corinthians* 15:45 St Paul says, 'The last Adam has become a life-giving Spirit.'

On the first Adam, of course, we project all the blame for our human predicament, for the originating taint of human disobedience, the apparently inborn waywardness that leads us humans off on our own foolish, selfish ways. Easter comes into it because the Second Adam, the raised Christ, is known as a life-giving Spirit that reverses our crooked and bent human nature.

Two thousand years since the birth of Jesus we gather in the first instance to remember him. Our remembering of him gives us our Christian identity, for nobody remembers him in precisely the way we do. Of course, we remember nothing at all about his physical appearance, his height, his weight, the shape of his nose or the colour of his eyes. Rather, when we say we remember him it is not so much things about him, but Jesus himself whom we remember, his essential character. What we remember is the uniquely rich texture of the distinctive love or self-giving that was incarnate in him and placarded before the world in all the events and incidents in which he acted and reacted.

By telling the Jesus story we remember the distinctively unconditional self-giving that ended in his being lifted up in awful beauty on the Cross. And it is our conviction that the Cross speaks more eloquently of the gracious, self-giving, love or Spirit of God than all the disputations of the Pharisees.

But we do not just *remember* the love or self-giving Spirit that was incarnate in Jesus. The nub of our Easter experience is that this unique and distinctive self-giving character that we remember we now *know*, not by description, but by actual acquaintance in the communion of the Church. The very same Spirit of Christ flows among us, informing and transforming our lives as a refreshing breath of life. We continue after two thousand years to make the claim that Christ was raised for our justification because we know his life-giving energy, his Spirit of love or self-giving, as that which repairs the ragged and frayed ends of our lives and thus straightens us out. This is why salvation is not something we do but something we receive.

There is another dimension of the justifying or straightening out of things by God which we ignore at our peril. Those of you who are familiar with the words of Handel's *Messiah* will remember that Handel worked with a text from *Isaiah*, embodying the saving promise of God, 'Every valley shall be exalted and every mountain and hill shall be made low.' The promise of God in relation to his dealing with the world is to even out the bumps, the high places and the low places, so as to smooth away the unevenness of things and straighten things out, by making the crooked straight and the rough places plain.

This straightening out imagery applies not so much to individual lives but to society as a whole. It embodies the promise of social equity, a more equal sharing not only of the world's resources, but also the distribution of well-being. There is a link between individual righteousness and social justice because, while salvation is not a matter of getting a tick for good works but the unmerited gift of God, it nevertheless leads to the doing of good works.

If one of the most significant ecumenical steps forwards in the last year has been the reversal of 450 years of hostility over the theological question of justification, a step which is injecting new life into the ecumenical movement, perhaps the most significant step forwards in the secular world has been the huge achievement, now openly acknowledged to have been largely achieved by the combined activity of Churches on the international level, in relation to the remission of unpayable Third World debt.

The United Kingdom, the United States and Canada have now committed themselves to 100 per cent remission of unpayable Third World debt. Japan, with a slightly different approach, is continuing to collect repayments but is putting the money it receives back into development projects in debtor countries. The International Monetary Fund and the World Bank are coming under increasing pressure to straighten out some of the most cruel inequities in the world between rich and abject poor. Australia's announcement that it will remit $18 million of loans through the World Bank for Third World countries is a ray of hope for the world this Easter and the Government is to be commended for it.

More people have been saved from poverty in the last fifty years than in the last 500. However, the population of the world has exploded, so there are proportionally many more who remain trapped in poverty than ever before. Of course, nobody supports the unconditional remission of Third World debt without questions of corruption and the siphoning off of money by ruling elites being addressed, or without attention being paid to the possible misuse of remitted debt repayments by increased spending on arms, or without a commitment to addressing pressing educational needs.

So the remission of debt has to be matched by positive programs to eliminate poverty. One of the next goals is to ensure that every child in the world has access at least to primary education by the year 2015. The fight against corruption and to promote education and development programs falls clearly within the brief of the Churches who are uniquely placed in the world to do just that.

We are not accounted and made righteous by our own human achievements but only by the free gift of God's gracious love. As our individual lives are straightened out and renewed by the gracious presence of the Spirit of the Easter Jesus, we find ourselves cooperatively working with God to help straighten out the problems of the world. We celebrate today because Christ died for our offences, but was raised for our justification, to straighten us all out.

28

In Boiling Oil

Preached in Christ Church Cathedral, Newcastle on
2 May 1999, on the occasion of the centenary of
St John's Theological College, Morpeth.

About a month ago, as I started to entertain some thoughts about what I might say here tonight, I found myself cutting down a tree.

It happened like this. My wife and I have a few acres of land in the south-western corner of Western Australia where eventually we plan to retire. Ours is one of four very small properties in a cleared pocket of state forest. Some of the forest trees grow very close to the house and my wife became worried about one dead Jarrah tree after it dropped a branch in a storm. I volunteered to cut it down. 'You know how to cut down a tree, do you?' she asked sensitively and with only the very slightest suggestion that this might not be a good idea. I replied with more confidence than common sense that I had learned this skill in the Boy Scouts.

As it happened this particular tree was somewhat more substantial than the small saplings on which we practised in the

Boy Scouts. It was about two feet in diameter at the bottom and at least fifty feet high. But the principles of tree-cutting should have worked just the same. So, using an electric chainsaw and drawing on the power supply from the nearby house, I cut out the first wedge, and I must say it came away beautifully. Then on the other side and a little higher up I put in the next cut to within half an inch or so of the gaping space where the first cut had been made. At this point I heard a crack, which was more or less what I expected. But, alas, instead of beginning to fall forwards in the direction of the first major cut, I found that the tree was actually leaning back, just a little, but sufficient to rest its full weight on the blade of the chainsaw so as to jam it there. There was no way of getting it out.

To make matters worse the atmosphere was unsettled and a little gusty, so that the tree was visibly swaying at the top as the trunk balanced back precariously on the jammed chainsaw. Moreover, the tree was teetering somewhat alarmingly in the direction of the house. Naturally, a sense of quickening panic and doom began to set in and the adrenaline began to pump. Boy, was I in boiling oil!

I shouted to my wife to phone the neighbours for help. One, an elderly chap called Ed, said he would bring some wedges to drive into the cut to tip the tree on its right way and so release the jammed chainsaw. Unfortunately, he succeeded only in compounding the panic. When I tell you that Ed is over seventy, has recently had four by-passes, been accidentally electrocuted a couple of times in his life and survived, and that he wears a pair of glasses with the lens entirely missing on one side, you might think that the prospect for help from that quarter may not have been great. But it wasn't because of the missing lens that he said with an air of gravity, 'This doesn't look too good.'

After the hammering of wedges into the cut made no

visible difference, he declared that he didn't think we were going to be able to do anything. 'It's too dangerous', he said. Of course it didn't look too good, and it was too dangerous, and I didn't need him to tell me so.

Ed suggested we had better phone the Department of Conservation and Land Management, known in Western Australia by the letters C–A–L–M – calm! I was reluctant to do this as it was their tree on their land that I was illegally cutting down. Boy, *was* I in boiling oil! In any event, CALM had no field officers on duty at weekends but volunteered to get somebody there the following Thursday. 'By that time the tree will have fallen on top of the house', I shouted down the telephone, as the level of agitation, and probably my blood pressure, rose.

By this time the neighbour on the other side had turned up. He was a younger and more adventurous chap, and was prepared to climb up a ladder precariously rested against the teetering trunk so as to hammer in a nail. The idea was to secure a chain high enough up to make it possible to winch the tree forwards so that it would fall in the right direction.

All this time the tree was swaying precariously around and I was only too aware that barely half an inch of timber attached it to the stump. Ed tightened up his winch and chain just a little, and then suggested that the wedges should now be hammered a little further into the cut so as to release the jammed saw. But as the three of us approached the tree to do this there was an almighty crack. Somebody yelled 'Watch out!' and we scattered in all directions as down came the tree with a walloping thump and a splintering shower of wood and branches and flying leaves.

Well, you will be relieved to know that the tree fell away from the house in the very direction I had intended in the first place. The pity was that I did not actually see it come down, and couldn't shout 'Timber!' as I had imagined I would, because I was too busy running in the opposite direction.

In the calm of relief that followed I began to ask myself why on earth I had been so crazy as to think I could simply cut down a tree, so large and so dangerously close to the house? And, as I processed the folly of this little public trauma, and sifted through my inner motives, it dawned on me that in preparation for tonight I had started a week or so earlier to read Peter Hempenstall's biography of Ernest Henry Burgmann. It was Burgmann who persuaded the clergy and people of the Diocese of Armidale to agree to the removal of St John's College to Morpeth in 1925. Once established at Morpeth, Burgmann then served as its Warden with great distinction for eight more years. Notwithstanding Arthur Vincent Green, its founder, this was undoubtedly the decisively formative period of St John's one hundred years of life.

Some years later, in the 1950s at Young, Burgmann, as Bishop of Canberra and Goulburn, confirmed me when I was about fourteen. I can still summon up a quite vivid picture of him sitting in the chair, bejowled and mitred, in that poignant moment just as I was about to kneel before him for the laying on of hands. Then in my own years at St John's as a theological student the college was staffed by two of 'Burgie's boys', Bob Davies and Gordon Griffiths. This was a time of renaissance, a flowering of the original Burgmann ideals in the College and renewed confidence – its halcyon days. Believe it or not there were seventy-seven students in my final year. So, in one way or another, Burgmann has been a very important direct and indirect influence in my life, as in the lives of so many others who revere him as one of the few genuinely great men of the Australian Church.

And this is where the Morpeth story connects with the felling of the tree. For I had reached the chapter which told of his bushman's life prior to ordination, when he worked as an axeman, felling tall timber and he learned the catechism and Greek vocabulary pinned to the trees he was cutting down. Clearly, the subliminal text ran something like this: 'The great Ernest Henry Burgmann used to cut down trees. Burgmann confirmed me and is something of a hero, an episcopal model for us all, and if Burgmann could do it, so can I.' Perhaps, indeed, what was operative was an underlying, unexpressed assumption that the ability to cut down trees was one of the seven gifts that passed from his axeman's hands at confirmation.

Certainly, in the long history of St John's College that we celebrate tonight, the axeman bishop stands head and shoulders above all others. He was effectively its founder at Morpeth not just in the sense that he was the one responsible for moving the College from Armidale, but insofar as he, with some like-minded colleagues, established what became known in the early 1930s as 'the Morpeth mind'.

There are a number of ingredients of 'the Morpeth mind' that make for a very distinctive institutional style and character.

Firstly, it involved an approach to the study of theology that was both catholic and critical, in contrast with the rather more conservative, naive biblicism or even hard-nosed fundamentalism, on offer elsewhere. A volume entitled *Essays Catholic and Critical* had been published in England in 1926, in which the authors promoted an open and critical approach to the study of the biblical texts and that was not averse to the idea that the human reason could be a vehicle of the revelation of divine truth.

Burgmann made the fundamental approach of *Essays Catholic and Critical* his own and he built it into the educational foundations of St John's in the crucial years between 1926 and 1933. He dreamed of a 'university in the bush' where theology would rub shoulders with the study of other disciplines, in the belief that the outcome would be a far more robust product than the usual insipid seminary fare which tended to content itself with introducing students to little more than a single and narrow theological tradition coupled with a style of churchmanship. Burgmann gave to St John's an approach to theological education designed to produce a mature approach to theology both progressively catholic and critical. I am sure this remains as part of the Morpeth mind today.

Secondly, prior to studying theology Burgmann had himself done a good deal of work at the University of Sydney in the then newly emerging science of human psychology. He introduced and interpreted the ideas of Freud to Australian audiences and worked at the interface between faith and human psychology, between concrete religious experience and the abstractions of theology. This led him to the clear view that the words of the Christian tradition which eventually found their way into the texts of scriptures, creeds and dogmatic definitions, started life as the verbal precipitate of religious experience. Revelation was not so much the words of the scriptural text in some abstract and absolute sense. Rather, the words of the scriptural texts represented the halting, feeble human attempt over a very long period of time to express at least something of a reality discerned in religious experience, but by definition beyond words.

Theology thus became the finite human attempt to encapsulate in verbal form something of the surpassing mystery of the Infinite, fleetingly glimpsed in the dynamic interpersonal relationship between God and people of faith. To wrestle with ambiguity in quest of a truth that is finally to be attained only at the end of a journey, rather than already possessed at its start, is the second basic ingredient of the Morpeth mind.

Then there was a third basic ingredient. 'The Morpeth mind' involved some serious reflection on the place of theological education as a positive force for good in the developing mind of a young, emergent nation. A firm belief in the importance of the theological and religious formation not just of priests but of the younger generation of Australians generally, was also one of Burgmann's life-long concerns. Long before contextual theology became popular in the 1960s Burgmann built into the theological foundations of the Morpeth mind a commitment to a self-consciously incarnational approach to Christianity in its local, national context. This meant theological and moral reflection on the country – its distinctive natural qualities and its social and political life.

Burgmann was committed to a robust engagement with the affairs of the nation, and actively worked at bringing the insights of theology and the values of the Gospel to public debate, particularly in the 1930s, after first-hand experience of the disastrous social effects of unemployment in the Hunter Valley following the Great Depression. More than once Burgmann found himself in hot water, when the adrenaline pumped and he found himself locked in sometimes heated controversy.

For those of us who have been closely associated with St John's a theology of political and social engagement does not entail getting oneself into hot water, as much as boiling oil. We are aware, as we celebrate the patronal festival of the College on 6 May, that the 1662 Prayer Book designates the day as the feast of St John *ante portam latinam*, when the focus is on the mythical incident in which St John is said to have been boiled in oil outside the Latin Gate for inciting public disturbance. As tradition has it, St John was delivered miraculously and unharmed.

Like so many myths the story encapsulates a timeless truth of our individual and corporate subconscious. When things do not go according to plan, when a situation of crisis envelops us and the adrenaline pumps, or when the heat is turned up and we find ourselves in the public firing line, we know the human experience of being in boiling oil. Emotionally and psychologically, we are probably in boiling oil more often than the apparent calm that outward circumstance might suggest.

Certainly, as a Church in recent times, we have found ourselves divided by the conflict of ideas – the ordination of women, euthanasia, lay presidency at the eucharist, the ordination of gay people in long-term committed relationships. When things have got a little out of our control and tempers have flared, sometimes with hand-wringing and foot-stamping, or when people have overreacted with more heat than light, we have found ourselves in boiling oil. The miracle is that by the forgiveness and grace of God we are enabled to extricate ourselves from such seething cauldrons.

But what is true of our experience from time to time as individuals and in the life of our Church is true also of contemporary life in our country as a whole. As one looks at the history of this nation, one can be forgiven for thinking that we have been in boiling oil for some time. And what is at stake is much more threatening and potentially destructive than a tree falling on a house. Temperatures have been rising over the republic, the issue of Native Title and the Ten Point plan, and the unthinkable threat of an election fought on issues of race.

We have witnessed resentment and anger over increased aged care charges, over the suppression of labour market programs in a time of high unemployment, and over the method of distributing welfare contracts in a privatised system. There is the issue of the reduction of funding for childcare facilities and for the care of those with disabilities.

We may as a nation emerge miraculously and unscathed from all this. But my conditioning by the Morpeth mind tells me otherwise. Indeed, as we celebrate 100 years of theological education at St John's College, this is the question. What can the Morpeth mind bring to this particular state of social and political affairs? Can a robust theology, progressively catholic and critical and prepared honestly to wrestle to discern where the truth lies and unreservedly committed to a thoroughly incarnational engagement with the world, continue to minister to the equal distribution of well-being and the achievement of national peace – bearing in mind that peace is a large and luxuriant tree, whose roots are justice? Can the Morpeth mind prepare us and strengthen us to risk the boiling oil of engagement with the political process that the Gospel so clearly lays upon us?

St Augustine once said to those about to be baptised in his cathedral church at Hippo in North Africa, 'Receive what you are and become what you receive.' Those of us who have received our formation at St John's College Morpeth in a distinctive theological mind must become what we have received. Tonight, indeed, we celebrate what we have received and rededicate ourselves to become what we celebrate.

29

LEO AND TAURUS

PREACHED AT THE DEDICATION AND CONSECRATION
OF THE CHAPEL OF ST MARK AND ST LUKE, WHITFORDS,
ON SUNDAY 19 SEPTEMBER 1999.

G.K. Chesterton once said that when people give up belief in God it is not that they then believe nothing. Rather, they tend to believe anything. As I drive around the city, listening to the car radio, I often think of this remark. On ABC 720 I regularly catch a little of a lunchtime segment in which the presenter talks on line with somebody called Mystic Medusa. Mystic Medusa purports to be able to give advice by reading the stars.

I was anxious to find out what our fortunes might be as we consecrate this new building. Will the message of the stars be favourable or fearsome? Somehow I failed to connect with Mystic Medusa so I had to content myself with the written version of the stars in the daily newspaper. When I looked up Leo the Lion it said, 'How long you put up with other people's nonsense is your decision. Are you going to sit calmly in the passenger seat while the driver's out of control? Perhaps you should think again.' Clearly, there is some urging here not to suffer fools gladly, an encouragement to be more assertive and aggressive and not sit calmly and be taken for a ride while things career out of your control. Well, I guess that is what we might expect of Leo the Lion – assertiveness to the point of aggression in order to get one's way, even if it means roaring at people and making them jump.

Then I looked up Taurus, the bull or ox, and the paragraph read: 'Watching an ant trying to climb the slopes of a sandhill can be very frustrating. Yet somehow, although slow and steady, the ant eventually gets there. Don't worry if things seem hard this week. Just keep going until you make it.' In other words, stick with it, persevere, just keep on, and you will get there in the end. Just what you might expect, not just of a little ant on an uphill slope, but of a placid hardworking ox, yoked to a plough and plodding on.

I very much doubt if this advice is actually read from the stars. But I do note that differences in mood and temperament seem to inform the advice respectively to those said to be born under the stars of Leo and those born under Taurus. The message of the placid ox has to do with holding on, keeping your domestic cool, persistence and forbearance. Leo the Lion expresses the opposite kind of character. It may be nice to keep the peace, and endure whatever life throws up but feel free to take control and don't hesitate to assert your authority. Let rip with a little of the wild side. When it seems necessary be king of the beasts, roar somebody up.

Now, you do not have to be expert at occult stargazing, to know that these are not just opposing stereotypes, but both aspects of our inner human make-up. Regardless of when in the course of a calendar year we may have been born there is probably a bit of both the plodding ox and the more aggressively fearsome lion in all of us. We all have within us that quiet, placid tendency to forbearance and tolerance, to hold on through thick or thin, regardless of the challenges that come our way. We also have within us that more fiery temper that gets a bit short with people from time to time and does not suffer fools gladly, that lion-like tendency occasionally to rip into those who annoy us. There is a placid domesticated ox and the more wild and fearsome lion in each of us. The art of living involves striking a balance and achieving some kind of integrity between putting up with things, turning the other cheek and just holding on in there, and getting really frustrated, irritated and aggravated to the point of assertively making our presence felt with a roar.

In the symbolism of the Christian tradition the four evangelists, who bequeathed to us the four Gospels, have been represented in graphic art by the four winged animals mentioned in the *Book of Revelation*. John is a winged eagle, Matthew a winged angel, Mark, the writer of the first Gospel, is the winged lion, and Luke is the winged ox or bull. It is the latter two that are of interest to us today, for this building that we are consecrating is designed to serve two institutions – the school under the patronage of St Mark and the parish under the patronage of St Luke. Today our interest falls on the lion and the ox.

I would not dare to push the analogy to suggest that those who belong to the community of the school are a bit on the wild side, inclined not to suffer fools gladly, but to assert themselves, roar and make their presence felt, while the placid Taurans of the community around about always turn the other cheek, knowing that this will be better for the sake of peace in the end. That kind of superficial stereotyping will not get us far.

Rather, it is more creative to suggest that what will develop in this building dedicated to St Mark and St Luke, is a kind of marriage of school and parish, the lion and the ox, in a joint venture.

It stuck me the first day I walked into this building when it was only partly constructed that one day the large roundels in the west wall, which today are temporarily filled with geometric coloured glass, might appropriately bear images respectively of the lion in one and the ox in the other.

And the marriage of these two institutions that will gradually make their home here, is not just a marriage of convenience, or a cost-cutting strategy for purposes of economic rationalism (even though it does not make much sense to have two separate buildings essentially the same, for the same purpose, in the same vicinity, when one will clearly suffice). Rather, a joint venture between school and parish is designed for the positive spiritual good of the mutual enrichment of both. Leo and Taurus invite us to think of complementary roles which produce a mutually enriching balance with an integrity of its own. And this may be more important than we might think.

In the Middle Ages, following the break-up of the Roman Empire when security forces were no longer around to keep the peace, the *pax romana*, the ensuing slump into social disorder meant that Christian civilisation only survived by the skin of its teeth. We speak of this period as the 'Dark Ages'. In that environment the embryonic parish system came under pressure and the enclosed monastic house came into its own. The monastic house became not only a secure place in which men and women respectively could live together cooperatively in community, but a place of education and learning in an otherwise dark age. In other words, the Church survived only with the structural help of a new kind of institution, whose mission in the world extended well beyond its own walls, for monastic houses became the springboard for educational and charitable work in the neighbouring community. Local people from the villages around about came to worship in great Abbey churches built within their walls.

Today we face an environment that is, in significant ways, not dissimilar from that following the break-up of the Roman Empire. There are signs that our society is becoming more fragmented, less secure, more and more violent and more drug-ridden, as traditional value systems break down. But the challenge is not so much a matter of insecurity, as secularism. The word 'secular' essentially means the present, the present age, and secularism is essentially a concentration on the immediate concerns of this world without a transcendent reference. We become secularised when we become immersed and absorbed in the present – beguiled by the demands and enticements of the present world of commerce and sport, exploiting the environment with no thought for tomorrow, and entertaining ourselves to death.

In this new and challenging environment, we cannot expect the traditional parish system to sustain Christian civilisation alone. By and large Sunday schools have become a thing of the past. Parish confirmations involve but a few. Youth work is minimal. Secular, worldly marriages are as common as those in church. We have a lot to do to turn things around.

Not every parish of the future will function in tandem with a school, but in this new environment schools, as centres for the transmission of Christian faith and the values of the Gospel, with school chapels functioning also as parish churches, are bound to become a more important factor.

The initial contact with a family that a school affords, that is to say, through the point of entry of caring for its children, has obvious advantages. Where the treasure is, there will the heart be also. Parents naturally treasure their children. Where they are the hearts of parents will also be. And we know that what goes on at home impacts upon a child's performance at school. With a little imagination the facilities of schools can provide continuing educational opportunities for adults as well as children. Clearly, a school is an obvious focal place for ministering to whole families.

When in the early 1980s we conceived the idea of establishing the first Anglican educational system in Australia, a network of schools with low fee structure to make them as accessible as possible to as many families as possible, and with a high degree of parental involvement, we quite deliberately called them *community* schools. St Mark's was the first of them. These new institutions were to be unequivocally schools of the Anglican community, designed to transmit the faith and values of the Gospel along with a quality education. But the word 'community' was understood to be deliberately ambiguous. It was meant to signal also a close association of the school with the neighbouring community. By using community facilities, such as local swimming pools, to avoid increasing the fee structure, and by offering its own facilities for wider community use and its talents for wider community enrichment, it would have a genuine community orientation. Community service and good citizenship are now par for the course in our school programs. The fact that we are consecrating a school chapel today that will also function as a parish church for the wider community also gives tangible expression to this original ideal.

In the context of the wider world this signals something to us of great importance. In the very word 'community', you can hear already the element of 'unity'. 'Comm-unity' is unity together with one another. In community there is human unity. We are essentially one – mutually inter-dependent rather than self-centred and essentially selfish, independent and autonomous units. And insofar as we can build real community, based on values of truth, unity, harmony and peace, we constitute a sign in this present secular world of the future dawning kingdom of God. In the unity of human community we bring to the world not just a transcendent reference, but a future-oriented reference and a hope that makes us dissatisfied with the world as it is in the present, which spurs us on to work for its transformation in justice and peace. That is what community service is all about.

The first reading from *Isaiah* 11:6–9 was chosen because it sets forward in poetic images a glimpse of the dawning kingdom of God, the object of our hope. The lion will lie down with the ox. Nature, which as Hobbes said, is 'red in tooth and claw', regularly warring and at enmity, will be tranquillised. Even a child will play on the hole of the asp and not come to harm. The lion will recognise its own more placid nature; on that day it will eat chaff. The vision of the kingdom is a vision in which warring factions lie down together. As the kingdom dawns among us we recognise aspects of ourselves, both placid and lion-like, in one another. As kindred spirits we commit ourselves to live together in community, in the balance of perfect harmony and peace.

The school's willingness to share the use of this building with the community of the parish is thus much more than an exercise of economic rationalism. It will assist the school to focus on the wider mission of the people of God in worship and service. The very same building will focus the parish on the importance of the family, on developing meaningful contact with children and their education in the discipline of Christ and the values of the Gospel. When you think about it, you cannot really have the one without the other.

This new building embodies a wonderful vision! May God pour the abundance of his blessing upon it.

30

CORPUS CHRISTI

PREACHED AT ST CHRISTOPHER'S CHURCH, CITY BEACH,
ON SUNDAY, 25 JUNE 2000.

Refrigerators tend to lead us into bad habits. Because they are designed for preserving food, food is often kept for much longer than it should be. But I don't think this happens intentionally.

This is because nobody has yet been able to design a refrigerator which allows you to see beyond the front few inches of the shelving. Inevitably, things in fridges get pushed to the back. When you can get nothing more in, and things are stacked one on top of the other, it is necessary to do a complete spring clean. Everything must be pulled out for the wash down with warm water and the mandatory dash of fragrant vanilla prescribed in the handy hints column of the *Women's Weekly*.

It is then that you find all sorts of bits and pieces – a shrivelled orange that must have got there last summer, some ends of cheese in plastic wrap that have hardened with time, a carton with an inch of milk in it (a little sour I am afraid) and, of course, the last few slices of a loaf of bread, still in the plastic wrapping paper but furry at the edges with patches of bluish mould.

I am sure my wife would want me to tell you that I am not drawing on my experience of life in the Carnley household, which is too well organised for all this to happen. I know about these things because of my experience of life in Queensland in the 1970s as Warden of a University College, which housed about 160 young men, and which boasted numerous refrigerators. Some were owned by the student club and were dotted around the college in dormitory kitchenettes, and others were privately owned, in student rooms. Either way, at the end of term they yielded a regular assortment of mouldy odds and ends. Like the sepulchres of the ancient world, they were regularly found to contain all manner of dried up and dead things.

I guess that, as refrigerators are relatively modern inventions, the human experience of finding mouldy bits and pieces was an even more common experience in the centuries before our time. Dead and mouldy bread would have been commonplace on the pantry shelves of the ancient world. And who would have thought, before the 1950s, that something related to mould on bread contained the source of life? For penicillin, as I understand it, is an extract of a kind of mould.

It is hard to imagine what medicine was like before the discovery of penicillin. It does not bear thinking about how many lives were lost. Ironically the cure was there all the time, imprisoned within a relative of the blue mould that sat for centuries upon the kitchen shelf. There it was, a hidden gift of God, waiting to be humanly accessed.

Of course, before penicillin there were substitutes. I remember being fed sulphur tablets during my time of national service training in the late 1950s, after I had contracted pneumonia. Sulphur tablets were not all that satisfactory as a cure. Apart from their size, which required you to make a regular meal of them, there was always the danger that the sulphur would recrystallise in one's kidneys. When taking them it was necessary therefore to drink enormous quantities of water. Nor was the sulphur the really sure-fire cure that penicillin proved to be.

St John, I suspect, imagined that the bread of life, the living bread that Jesus gave, would not so much cure disease as prevent death. For we hear in *John's Gospel*, 'Whoever eats this bread will never die.' In the ancient world there were many religious movements that held out the hope of avoiding the trauma of death by consuming the food of immortality. Some early Gnostic sects (called Gnostic because they promised the initiate a secret, non-rational knowledge not available to anybody else) denied the resurrection as a future occurrence beyond the grave, for example, because they believed that they had already gained access to the secret of life. Because they enjoyed an experience of new life and immortality this side of the grave, they denied the need for resurrection. They believed they would never die. This meant that they would avoid the trauma of death – there would be no experience of the grave at all.

If *John's Gospel* was written in a Gnostic environment, as many scholars now think, this may explain why John used the term 'the bread of life', and also the saying that 'whoever eats this bread will live for ever'. John, in other words, may have been responding to the challenge to communicate with his audience, as we all must do, by using their language to interpret the meaning and significance of Jesus as the Christ. In the other Gospels, the phrase 'bread of life' does not occur at all.

Writing early in the second century, St Ignatius of Antioch, whose letters are said to have a stylistic affinity with

John's writing, speaks of the eucharistic bread as 'the medicine of immortality' and appears to mean a similar thing. The food that Jesus gave supplied nourishment for life without end. Perhaps the suggestion of immortality attaching to the bread of the eucharist also lies behind Paul's warning that those who participate in the eucharist unworthily will get sick and die. In reprimanding those who were failing to discern and reverence the Lord's body by treating the eucharist as a mundane banquet, he wrote, 'For this reason many of you are weak and ill, and some have died' (1 Corinthians 11:30). Can it be that there was at first some kind of belief that the bread of life that Jesus gives, properly discerned and worthily and reverently consumed, contained the secret of immortality?

After 2000 years of the Christian experience of death, its harsh and uncompromising reality and apparent finality, we can hardly maintain the belief that the bread of life helps us Christians to avoid sickness and death and the trauma of the grave. Nor, these days, do we necessarily believe that the eucharistic bread *contains* some secret inner substance, somehow hidden behind the outward form and texture and taste of bread, which may be said to preserve our souls for ever. There is no spiritual penicillin hidden there still waiting to be scientifically discovered.

Naturally enough, the Church has sometimes felt it necessary to develop theories to explain how it is that the bread of the eucharist is not just bread, but also the body of Christ. And so, in the Middle Ages, under the influence of Thomas Aquinas who popularised the use of Aristotelian categories of thought, it became fashionable to speak of 'transubstantiation'. It was as though, while the bread continued to look and taste like bread, there was a secret inner change of substance somehow deep inside the bread, so as to enable the faithful somewhat mechanically to receive the Body of Christ.

These days we tend to feel that language referring to an inner change of substance is a little too static, and that while once Christians tended to speak as though the Body of Christ were a static substance *contained* in the bread, it would be more appropriate to speak in more dynamic language. Instead of speaking of the Body of Christ *contained in* the bread, it is suggested that we might think of the Body of Christ *conveyed by* the taking, the blessing, the breaking and the sharing of the bread.

Let me give you an example to illustrate the difference. Imagine a local supermarket with a number of boxes of chocolates on a shelf. In comes a lover who selects one and purchases it to present as a gift to his beloved. He takes it home, carefully removes the price label of course, and wraps the box of chocolates in coloured paper. He takes it to the home of his beloved. He rings the bell, just a little sheepishly, with the box in his hand behind his back. When the door is opened he presents, with a flourish, his box of chocolates.

Now in a sense, that particular box of chocolates has taken on a meaning and significance that makes it quite different from the other boxes of chocolates that remain on the supermarket shelf. For a start it is no longer just *a* box of chocolates but *his* box of chocolates. This particular box of chocolates has been endowed with new meaning and significance by being given and received within the context of a loving relationship. Indeed, the box of chocolates is not just a sign of the lover's affection and love for the beloved, it actually conveys these spiritual realities. Love is actually expressed and conveyed within the dynamic of the interpersonal relationship.

Now we would not say that the lover's love was somehow *contained in* the chocolates. It would not be possible to take the chocolates, empty them on a table, dissect them with a knife and probe about in the strawberry cream and praline fillings to try and find a hidden substance called 'love'. Substance is the wrong kind of category. It is not that the lover's love is a substance, somehow contained in the chocolates. Nevertheless it is without doubt a spiritual reality conveyed by the chocolates. This happens as a kind of event precisely when the chocolates are brought in a particular way within the dynamics of an interpersonal relationship and presented as a gift from the lover to the beloved.

In the same way the Body of Christ may not be found as a hidden substance, somehow inside the bread of the eucharist. But when some bread is set apart from other bread and consecrated by being taken within the fourfold action of the taking, blessing, breaking and sharing by the people of God, it conveys the spiritual reality of Christ's very own life and presence. For us the living bread which Jesus gives is in faith perceived and received as a sign of his giving of himself. He is not contained in, so much as conveyed by, the action of taking, blessing, breaking and sharing of the bread. So our language these days becomes less static, more dynamic.

We can also begin to discern something of what Jesus means when he takes bread and says, 'This is my body' if we think about why our bodies are important. The unique physical tokens of our bodies allow others to recognise us. Through our bodies we communicate with one another, speaking with our vocal chords and hearing with the auditory system of our ears. Through our bodies we have access to one another – we hug and embrace. And when we take ourselves overseas others' access to us is at least limited if not denied because of the physical removal of our bodies.

Over the last few weeks since I became Primate, I have been asked on numerous occasions about the whereabouts of Jesus' resurrection body. In particular, where was the raised Jesus between the appearances? Hostile fundamentalist sectarians, who find it difficult to think in any other way but the very literal, seem to be anxious to assimilate Jesus' resurrection with any other event to history and make it as plain as the nose on your face. They suggest that at the resurrection Jesus simply sat up, rubbed his eyes and then made his way out of the tomb, to resume life on this mundane plane. It has actually been asserted in an article on one web page that Jesus was restored to this world like Lazarus. The implication seems to be that between various appearances he was holed up somewhere, perhaps in the Jerusalem caravan park.

A less fundamentalist, and I would say far more orthodox Christian understanding of things, would suggest that the resurrection was not a mere resuscitation or restoration to life in this world, but essentially a transformation. At the resurrection Jesus' body was transformed into a heavenly body or, as St Paul said, a spiritual body rather than a terrestrial body, and his appearances were revelatory, transcendent appearances from the radical hiddenness of God. Thus, St Paul speaks of the heavenly vision of the raised Christ, rather than someone available to anyone who rolled up to inspect and scrutinise.

The Gospel traditions also point to the more transcendent or heavenly type of appearance, given that Jesus appears to disciples mysteriously, behind closed doors, and then disappears. He miraculously vanishes after his encounter with disciples on the Road to Emmaus, for example. I honestly do not think he just slipped out for a breath of fresh air. Rather, the text suggests a heavenly transformed and glorified Christ, whose existence is to be thought of on a transcendent and eternal and not just a mundane plane. We need to be more imaginative, less literal in our reading of these Biblical traditions.

Had St Paul been asked the question, 'Where is the body of Christ?', I think he would have replied with a simple and somewhat startling answer. He would have said that the body of Christ is in two places, which are really one place – 'on the altar and around the altar'. For when St Paul speaks of the 'Body of Christ' he uses the term to refer to the bread of the eucharist and the people of God who gather and participate in the eucharist.

Now if our bodies are important for allowing others access to us, then what Paul means is that access to Christ is through the eucharistic bread – the Body of Christ – or through interpersonal communion with his people because the Church is the Body of Christ. Both holy bread and holy people give access to Christ and that is why either can be spoken of as the Body of Christ.

Certainly, we know that those who eat this bread, while they certainly do not avoid the trauma of death, nevertheless live for ever. This bread is the true and living bread, the medicine of immortality, because the life of the one to whom it allows us access is the eternal heavenly one, the one who invites us into the eternal divine communion of persons of the Blessed Trinity in one unity of being.

When we, through the sharing of a common life in communion have access to Christ through the Church, the Body of Christ, we have access to the communion of love that is timeless and eternal. We are not frozen or refrigerated, but animated. Not just preserved and stored, but transformed and made new. For the spiritually invigorating new life of Christ is actually known in experience to have been conveyed to us in the dynamic action to taking, blessing, breaking and sharing of bread. This bread is 'the Body of Christ, the Bread of Heaven'.

31

THE VALE OF SOUL MAKING

PREACHED IN ST GEORGE'S CATHEDRAL, PERTH ON 24 OCTOBER 1999 TO COMMEMORATE NATIONAL BREAST CANCER DAY.

My wife and I have a very small block of land down at Nannup, a whole thirteen acres, where eventually we hope to retire. At present it is a matter of getting the place in liveable order and of pruning a little broken-down orchard back into productivity. In the middle of the block there is a natural depression where someone in time past bulldozed to form a pond. Over the summer of 1998–9 I built a small dam wall out of rocks at the out-flow so as to raise the level of the water by about two feet. As a consequence, in the winter of 1999, with its added expanse of water, the pond became the home for all kinds of bird life, much more than usual. At one point we were visited by two black swans for about three weeks. But others have come for a more permanent stay.

Among these last spring was a pair of splendid ducks which the Australian Bird Guide has allowed us to identify as Mountain Ducks. Both male and female are predominantly blackish brown with white flashes on their wings. The male has a white ring around the neck, a bit like a clerical collar, and wears a splendid beige-coloured waistcoat. They make a very distinctive honking noise, with different levels of pitch distinguishing the cry of the male and the female.

After they had been around for a while we wondered if they would stay and breed. Then on one occasion we noticed with delight that they were accompanied on the water by nine fluffy ducklings. On the next visit, however, there were sadly only six, and on the visit after that, five. We wondered if this was just the result of a natural attrition or whether something had been getting them; a fox perhaps, though the area has been well baited by the Department of Conservation and Land Management to get rid of foxes.

But then the mystery was solved. We were startled one morning by a rumpus of honking and splashing and squawking, and we dashed out to see a huge Wedge-Tailed Eagle. On any reckoning it was a magnificent if fearsome creature, orange-tan in colour with a majestic wing span. But it was not coming in for the kill on a fixed flight path to snatch away a little duck in its tendons in the classic way to which David Attenborough has introduced us. Rather, the eagle itself was in some distress. It was weaving and turning in the air over the pond and the ruckus was being kicked up by a troupe of very lively crows, crying out and dive-bombing and pecking at it. This feathers-flying sky show lasted for one or two tense minutes before the eagle was eventually driven off.

I instinctively, though in retrospect somewhat comically, dashed to the support of the crows by grabbing a broom and waving it in the air and yelling 'sh-o-o!' to the eagle, even though I was quite a distance away and really entirely out of the action. This episode of defensive action on the part of the crows happened on two occasions, and on both the eagle flew off in retreat without taking any of the little ducks. Eventually they grew too large to constitute a continuing temptation.

I must say that I have never been enamoured of crows despite the useful garbage removal service they provide along the sides of country roads, but now I have a different view of them. It now strikes me that this little experience of the natural life of our planet is an acted parable of the way life is. The tranquil world of the pond, the life-sustaining water, and the enchanting charm of the life cycle, has its shadow side.

I have to concede that the eagle was probably looking for food to sustain its own young in a nest in some far-off tree, for that is the way the food chain works, and the eagle cannot therefore be condemned. Certainly, the world in which we live is one in which an inexorable principle operates that demands the sacrifice of life that others may live. That awesome and sobering truth occasionally surfaces in our own consciousness when we reflect on the source of the veal or the lamb on our plate. It is enough to drive some to be vegetarians. But that attempt at problem avoidance is only partially successful, for even when we pull a carrot or cut a lettuce, the same principle, though admittedly less poignant in its impact upon us, still operates – one form of life is sacrificed in order that another may live. That is the way our world is. The world is shot through with sacrifice, and an awareness of the tragic sense of life is never far away from our experience.

We might wish that it were otherwise, but further reflection coupled with a sense of realism may lead us to the conviction that this may in fact be the best of all possible worlds, even with its shadow side. For it is also a principle of the world we inhabit that no two objects can occupy the same place at the same time and that also means that tragedies do happen, as we regularly know to be the case from the carnage on our roads.

Of course it is thinkable that God could have made the world otherwise. It is thinkable that our world could be a soft world in which nothing tragically serious ever happens. God could have set things up so that every time there was danger of collision he could zoom in to hold objects competing for the same space apart. Perhaps motor vehicles could suddenly lose power so as never to bump into each other with force, and boiling water could suddenly become cold in order not to scald, and fire could suddenly lose its heat so as never to burn, knives could suddenly become blunt so as to lose their capacity to cause harm. The problem with such a world is that any regular sense of order would entirely disappear – natural regularities would be so often interrupted that science would be an impossibility.

It would also be a world in which we humans would never have to exercise any care or responsibility, for no matter what we did or how foolish or wantonly gross our behaviour, there would always be an intervention to prevent harm from being caused.

Moreover, apart from the fact that there would be no need to exercise any duty of care and responsibility, there would be no need for compassion, no need for love, no need, indeed, for the exercise of any of the virtues that we most admire – courage, fortitude, patience, persistence, heroism, the service and care of those in need – no need for our human nature to rise above itself. But, if God has created us to grow as human beings to spiritual and moral maturity, the world must be, not an entirely soft world devoid of challenges or difficulties, but a world in which challenges have to be met and hardships have to be overcome.

Hard though it may be for us from time to time, this may be the best of all possible worlds if there are to be possibilities for us to make moral choices and to grow to human maturity. The world is, in this sense, a vale of soul making.

The challenges that life-threatening diseases pose to us, that interrupt and disturb the tranquillity of our lives, are also part of the defective fallenness of the world, its shadow side. They pose challenges of a spiritual kind to those who must come to terms with them, but also to those who rise to their support and care. They pose challenges of a moral kind to health services and governments who must make right decisions about the allocation of resources for human well-being, as well as challenges to medical researchers and scientists. Would to God that more of the world's resources had been put into medical research than into the development of nuclear weaponry or the building of casinos. By now we might have been even further down the track towards some significant cures than we are. But the making of right decisions must involve some sacrifice. This includes some sacrificing their own interests and agendas in order that others may live.

That is the first line of reflection that arises for me out of the encounter of the eagle and the ducks, particularly on this day when we focus on the work of those who live with breast cancer and those who are dedicated to alleviate their suffering.

The second is this. Somehow the crows came to the support and defence of the little ducks, as a kind of protective, peace-keeping force, so as to hunt the eagle away. I suppose it is too much to think of this as a conscious decision of the crows. In all probability they simply knew by instinct that the eagle was a natural enemy. No doubt the protection of their own young, rather than of the ducks, was the motivating influence behind their determination to drive it from their territory. Yet, as it worked out, there was a whole cooperative enterprise operating here in favour of the survival of the little ducks. In a sense the whole community came out in support of them, even to the point where I myself instinctively found myself waving my broom and yelling 'sh-o-o!' And perhaps this helps us to understand what we are doing today. We come to the prayerful support of those who live with illness, particularly life-threatening illnesses, and we come automatically and instinctively. We do not have to sit down and think about it and decide whether we should do so or not. As T. S. Eliot said in his poem *Little Gidding* in *The Four Quartets*:

> You are not here to verify,
> Instruct yourself, or inform curiosity
> Or carry report. You are here to kneel
> Where prayer has been valid.

Somehow, the impulse to cry out to what lies beyond our immediate experience of life is built into us as an instinct. It is the valid instinct of prayer. And when we hit our thumb with a hammer and cry out 'Oh, God!' that is probably as much a prayer as a blasphemy. For all prayer is an instinctive cry in distress when we are at the limit of our own resources. We do not have to stop and think about it and reason why; there is simply nothing else we *can* do. 'Needs', said Thomas Traherne, 'are the ligatures that tie us to God.' When we cry out in need that is an archetypal prayer of petition.

True, we Christians craft the language into sonorous, rounded phrases in our written prayers and collects, but all intercessory prayer nevertheless is essentially a cry, a cry to God to be with us in our human struggle to overcome all that destroys the goodness and beauty of life. The impulse to pray for those who are ill arises instinctively, spontaneously and immediately within us.

And in a sense the parable of the crows, the eagle and the ducks speaks of the whole community coming out in mutual support to confront a common enemy. That is why we are here this evening, and it may be more important than we think. For it is the instinctive and spontaneous show of mutual support that leads with further reflection, in less heated emotion-charged moments, to a more sustained moral commitment, as when we sit down to address problems and to devise strategies to overcome our troubles. We instinctively cry to God to help us to overcome all manner of causes of human distress and tragedy and that is valid in itself. But it always leads to action, as the God of hope works in us cooperatively to achieve his intended purposes. Indeed, he knows our needs before we ask and the gift of his love is the initiating influence of our good works. The immediate instinctive cry for help when we cry out in need to what lies beyond our own limited human resources and the more sustained and considered determination to work for the redress of human suffering and distress go together – one feeds and nourishes the other.

And so we gather this evening to mark national Breast Cancer Day in solidarity, in a display of community support, to encourage those who live with disease and particularly those who are coming to terms with life-threatening disease, and to cheer on those in medical research who are making such positive gains in the treatment of all kinds of diseases.

We applaud those who sacrifice other possible preoccupations and concerns in order to concentrate their energies on this area of endeavour, that others may live. We celebrate the vital work of those who provide medical attention and care in our hospitals and hospices. We call on God to be our help and comfort in this joint endeavour of the whole community, as we at the same time call on governments to allocate increased resources to treatment and care and medical research, so as to drive disease ultimately away. All this we do spontaneously and instinctively, motivated by the validating impulse of love alone, which is the gracious presence of God with and within us.

32

PRIMATIAL INAUGURATION

PREACHED IN ST ANDREW'S CATHEDRAL, SYDNEY
ON SUNDAY 30 APRIL 2000.

In the northern autumn of 1562 an Antwerp cloth merchant was unpacking a consignment of cloth which had recently arrived from Turkey. In among the bales of cloth he found a small brown paper package, which he assumed must have been sent as a gift from the fabric supplier. On opening the package he found it contained some strange-looking smallish onions. Some he planted in his vegetable garden next to his cabbages in the hope of producing a crop next year. The rest he roasted and seasoned with oil and vinegar and then ate for his supper. Next spring, to his amazement, the onions in the garden bloomed as, yes, you will have guessed, tulips. These are believed to be the first to flower in Europe, in the spring of 1563.

This is an incident with which Ann and I can resonate, because when the mania began for us, our bulbs had to be refrigerated in brown paper packets to give them the experience of a northern European winter. Eight weeks or so of cold storage is needed to trigger the internal chemical changes between sugar and starch necessary to make them bloom. Long before our supply of bulbs grew to our present 2000, I was firmly given orders to vacate the kitchen refrigerator and buy my own, which I have done. But in the early days we lived with a low-grade anxiety about whether or not our precious bulbs might inadvertently make their way into a beef bourguignon.

For the last couple of years Ann and I have been taking the advice of the Council for Positive Aging seriously by working out in advance how we see ourselves spending our retirement. I have to tell you that in the week or two before the primatial election on 3 February I received both my ABN number for GST purposes as a small business operator as well as a licence number from the Nannup Shire Council as an owner-builder, to allow me to put up an extension to the little house. A radical change of plans, however, and genuine newness of life, has clearly overtaken us, so we must push thoughts of retirement to Stillpoint Tulip Farm a little further into the background.

But, why am I speaking so personally? It is because the ministry of a Primate, and indeed, any form of episcopal and priestly ministry, is in the first instance personal. It is the ministry of a person. We are not convinced as Anglicans that the shepherding ministry of pastoral oversight can effectively be exercised by a group or a committee. It is the ministry of a person, often in one-on-one ministry, with his or her particular interests and agendas, and with all the foibles and frailties too, that are necessarily brought to the task.

And, speaking personally, it means a huge amount to me and to my family to have so many of you who are our personal friends from so far back and from so far away here today to support us. Woody Allen once said that life for ninety per cent of the time is just a matter of turning up to things. Believe me, I am very encouraged and grateful for all of you who have gone out of your way to turn up today.

But this service today marks more than just the new ministry of a person. This happens to be the first representative gathering of leaders, both lay and ordained, of our national Church since the beginning of the new millennium. The focus should not just be on a person but on the opportunity it gives us for the renewal of our national Church life. Indeed, that is a second reason for speaking about the tulips. For had St Paul been a Dutchman living in the seventeenth century, searching for explanatory images to communicate something of the surpassing mystery of Easter faith as he wrote *I Corinthians* 15, he might well have said that when a bulb is placed in the ground and buried, it to all intents and purposes disappears from view and dies. But then, through the hidden mystery of the creative activity of God it blooms, a 'thin clear bubble of blood' dancing in the breeze.

At Easter we celebrate the bloom of new life, the mystery of the renewal of our life in Christ. It is a time for baptisms and for many of us it is the time for the renewal of our ordination vows. As you look at us bishops assembled in the cathedral today I guess, if we are honest, your first thought may come in the form of a question: Can these dry old bulbs live?

At first glance it may seem that the Church is a gerontocracy but I hasten to say that some of these onions are in fact already retired. And if you look more closely you will see some bright young faces beginning to emerge so it is not quite so desperate as it may at first appear. I can assure you that when these chaps are out of the rig they are in today, and when they are not standing in the traditional attitude of prayer with arms outstretched in the classic standing (*orans*) position leading worship, their hands will be more characteristically in the ten-to-two position as they drive their cars backwards and forwards and up and down the length and breadth of this nation.

We have the research officers of the premier of New South Wales to thank for the discovery that the first official use of the title 'Australia' in Australian history was in 1836 when William Grant Broughton was made the first 'Bishop of Australia'. There were at the time no cities. Sydney only became a city in 1842. In 1836 Broughton's See was the whole of Australia. Since then Australia has been sub-divided into its present twenty-three dioceses, served by a college of bishops and assistant bishops whose dedicated and heroic pastoral ministry covers the whole land. As a national Church we are very conscious that the marginalised are not only the poor and socially deprived or ethnic groupings of disadvantage but also the geographically isolated, the lonely and those who feel that the rest of the nation is neglecting them. Working out how to minister effectively in the neglected rural and isolated parts of Australia with properly trained non-stipendiary clergy is an important item on our current agenda.

It is a standing zoological joke that the Primate is the missing link. But in a sense that is true, at least insofar as he is supposed to be a link person, to facilitate the gathering and the deliberating and the decision making, with an originating role in relation to the corporate prayer and the thinking and the work of the group. It is a great privilege to have been asked to be of service in this kind of way, to this splendid body of dedicated men in this national work. Thus, today we are conscious that while primatial ministry is personal, it is also collegial, a ministry that is exercised as first among equals, in unity with others.

A Primate is also the link person with the other provinces of the Anglican Communion, particularly those of this immediate region. I am very grateful to colleagues from New Zealand, New Guinea, Melanesia, Myanmar, South East Asia, Hong Kong, and representatives of the Primates of Japan, the Philippines and the United States for taking the trouble to come today from so far away to remind us of our greater international belonging. Written expressions of support have come from Korea, Sri Lanka, India and Southern Africa. Since the recent international Primates' meeting in Portugal I count them already to be friends, and we are acutely conscious of our mutual interdependence, and our responsibilities and obligations to one another in an international communion of Churches.

Primatial ministry is personal, it is collegial. By now those of you who know the 1982 Lima Report on *Baptism, Eucharist and Ministry* of the Faith and Order Commission of the World Council of Churches will have realised that I am working with its threefold categorisation of ordained ministry, and especially today episcopal ministry, as personal, collegial and communal. For the ministry of a bishop, including the bishop in a primatial role, is not just personal and collegial but exercised in relation to the whole community of the Church – bishops, clergy and people together – as the whole people of God in their mission and ministry to the wider community of society.

As we relate to Australian society as a whole, all Churches at present have a clear evangelistic task to connect and re-connect with vast numbers of increasingly secularised Australians with whom we have lost touch. In the context of the tragic brokenness of the present world we also have responsibilities to foster dialogue with other faiths. We Christians certainly know that we have to look at ourselves and what we have to offer, how we are performing and how we can better work together. For we know perfectly well that we must be one that the world may know what kind of God our God is in terms of the unity and harmony of love and the ultimate relationality of persons. Clearly, we all have a task to do in terms of communication if the census figures relating to religious adherence in this country are to be turned around.

For all that, we have to remember that Jesus himself taught his disciples to think of themselves as a minority, doing a representative or priestly job for the whole, as salt in the stew and yeast in the dough. It is not the task of salt to turn the whole stew into more salt or of yeast to turn the whole lump of dough into more yeast, but rather to give some added flavour to the whole and to raise up the quality of community life. In the work of proclaiming in words and deeds the dawning kingdom of God, success is not therefore measured in numbers alone, though the proportion of the active agent in relation to the whole has, of course, to be adequate for the task. But how do we conceive the task of being salt and yeast? I want to make two points.

First, something about leadership. In 1990 Vaclav Havel, addressing the United States Congress, spoke of what Czechs and Slovaks had to learn from the capitalist West, following the humiliating collapse of eastern block economies. But he also said that he believed they had learned something from experience that they could teach us:

> The specific experience I am talking about has given me one certainty. Consciousness precedes being, and not the other way around, as the Marxists claim.

The Marxists mistakenly thought, he explained, that if you get the outward material circumstances of human being right, then right thought, right values, right morality, right human relationships and right culture would follow. That was, he said, both the essence of the Marxists' program and their fundamental mistake. And it is something for us to learn, for in a curious inversion of dialectical materialism we currently often hear the view expressed that if we can get the economy right, then everything else will fall happily into place. Thus, Aboriginal people are told that what they need is housing and health services and all will be well. There is no doubt in my mind that better housing and vastly improved health services are certainly needed, but something else is missing, something to do with consciousness – right fundamental attitudes, generosity of spirit, an open preparedness to acknowledge and honour original custodianship of the land, and to own the many injustices of dispossession. In a word 'spirituality' is the essential nub of the matter. Havel continued:

> For this reason the salvation of this human world lies nowhere else than in the human heart, in the human power to reflect, in human meekness and in human responsibility. Without a global revolution in the sphere of human consciousness, nothing will change for the better in the sphere of our being as humans, and the catastrophe towards which this world is headed – be it ecological, social, demographic or a general breakdown of civilisation – will be unavoidable.

If consciousness precedes being and not the other way around, then for those of us with responsibilities of leadership, matters of outward style may not be so important – whether leadership should be exercised from out front or from behind, or dressed up in one way rather than another. What is important is that leadership should be exercised from within.

Secondly, something about citizenship. The entire world at the moment seems to be disenchanted with leaders, it is shadowed by disillusionment and disappointment. Within our own shores and in this South East Asian region a similar despondency is in the air. Those in leadership positions do not appear to be delivering the goods in the way we expect. We wring our hands and complain. Why doesn't so and so do something about x or y or z? Since the Primatial election on 3 February I have received a lot of unsolicited advice through the mail about a wide range of issues. Indeed, it has become clear that many think of a Primate as a Mr Fixit. The expectations are enormous.

But if we think that way we delude ourselves and the truth is not in us. Perhaps it's time to swing the focus from leadership to citizenship, and perhaps the leader's chief communal role is to encourage people generally to ask some simple questions. What can I do in my place, my street, my block to build networks of love and neighbourly care? Without waiting on leaders to do things, what can I do to build a civil society right where I am? How can we enter more fully into community life in this locality with a little creative imagination so as to re-claim our hope?

There is an enormous difference between genuine hope and wishful thinking. Hope, in contrast to wishful thinking, is grounded in positive experiences which convince us we can go on and do better. We can give an account of the hope that is in us. And perhaps it is time not to get hooked on the many dispiriting problems that weigh us down, but instead to rekindle community commitment and participation by reflecting a little on the good things of the path along which we have come together. 'O God, we have heard with our ears, our Fathers have told us what wondrous things you have done in times of old'. Appreciative enquiry, reflection on the positives, identifying where there is already energy for change, may be a better way forwards.

Let me give you two examples that speak to me of new hope. The first has to do with the struggle of the people of Fitzroy in Melbourne to keep their local swimming pool in the face of a governmental decision to close it on the basis of the economic rationalist principle that, though providing an important community service, it did not pay. The imminent threat of closure mobilised the people of the Fitzroy community to make a noise. 'You can go down to the neighbouring Collingwood swimming pool', they were told. And so they did. Can you imagine – one thousand of them all trying to get into the Collingwood pool at the same time! The result? The Fitzroy pool is still there but the government is not. This was its first major public defeat, which signalled worse to come. There is an important message in there somewhere. For me it is that our best contribution as leaders may be to help people in local communities re-vision and re-claim their own destiny, so as to unleash wellsprings of creative imagination and hope across the land.

And hope arises in the most unlikely places. A remarkable priest from Chicago named Bliss Browne is the founder and director of a social transformation program entitled *Imagine Chicago* and is helping us launch a similar, through in our case statewide program, *Imagine WA*. In the Cathedral on Maundy Thursday she told the story of her niece who suffered an unexplained paralysis at the age of 16. When she was 17 years old she went to a Lutheran Youth Convention and was sitting on the sidelines in her wheelchair at a dance. At one point a young man came up to her and asked, 'Would you like to dance?' 'Yes', she said. It was a courageous choice; she might have said no. He wheeled her wheelchair into the centre of the dance floor and then went and got a chair and put it in front of her and sat on it. And then they held hands, shoulders and arms moved to the rhythm of the music, and – sitting in their chairs – they danced. Another young man noticed this and went and got another girl in a wheelchair and did the same thing. And the miracle was that in a matter of a few minutes every one of those teenagers on the entire dance floor was sitting on a chair – dancing. The re-kindling and re-claiming of hope happens in the most unlikely of places.

When we Christians give an account of the fundamental hope that is in us, and touch down on the high points of the journey over which we have come, it takes us back to the story of the empty tomb. Over its door we read the affirmative banner, 'Even where there is death there is hope.' And from the tomb we dare to hope that in the good purposes of God it is possible for the whole world to bloom.

33

J2K: The Millennium of the Incarnation of God

Preached in St George's Cathedral, Perth
on Christmas Day, 25 December 2000.

As I drove through the city on Tuesday of last week I heard an interview on the radio with a man whose business had to do with the naming rights of stars. Astronomers identify stars and then refer to them only by the mathematical coordinates of their positions in galaxies. Apparently it is now possible to give names to particular stars, which are registered by copyright in Washington and published in books placed in libraries around the world.

The person owning the naming rights receives a certificate and a booklet outlining procedures for locating his or her own particular star in the night sky. There is no need of 'the dish' for there are plenty of stars comparatively close at hand that can be seen with a domestic telescope. Indeed, because there are millions and millions of stars in the heavens, there is an almost unlimited supply of this unusual but very marketable commodity. The person being interviewed was at pains to point out that it was not that the star itself was being purchased, but only the naming rights. There was no suggestion that it might arrive in the post by express delivery. One simply purchases the right to give a star the name of one's choice. And all this for only $220.

He reported that the giving of names to stars was becoming particularly popular as a Christmas or Valentine Day's gift. He then went on to say, more seriously, that his special interest was to promote the naming of stars as a project of the Starlight Children's Foundation, which sees a particular value in the naming of stars after children who have died. He pointed out that this had a remarkably therapeutic role to play in the grieving process of parents and siblings. When a star is named after a deceased child, he said, it is very comforting for parents to be able to look up into the starry night sky and know that their child is 'up there', safely in heaven as it were.

What struck me about this interview was not so much the novelty of the entire idea, but the very natural tendency to identify a named star with the continuing heavenly existence of a deceased child. During the interview the words, 'knowing that he is up there in heaven', were repeated a number of times. There seemed to be a need to place a deceased child, in something more than a merely imaginative way, in a physical location identified by mathematical coordinates and the names of galaxies. It is as though we are still wedded to the idea that God's protective eternity lies literally somewhere in the heavens high above us.

Today we are celebrating the two thousandth anniversary of the birth of Jesus Christ. And for all the astronomical interest in the story of the Christmas star which guided the wise men, and which we still symbolically place on the top of our Christmas trees, one of the chief points of our celebrating over this last two thousand years has had to do, not with the heavenly remoteness of God somewhere above the starry sky, but with his earthly closeness. The message of Christmas is God *with* us, the God of love in whom we live and move and have our being. In the person and work of the human Jesus we become intimately aware of a God who is near at hand, who is both *by* our side and also *on* our side, as we struggle to live life well, in harmony and peace, in the face of all that spoils its goodness and beauty.

Nevertheless, there is a natural and apparently incurable human tendency to push God away, back into a heaven high above and away from us. This even conditions the way we think of the Incarnation. It can be suggested, for example, that prior to the Incarnation God was somehow absent from this world, like an absentee landlord, who 'came down from heaven' to dwell on this earth both *for a time* and for the *first* time, in the person of Jesus Christ.

Sometimes we imagine the celebration of the Incarnation of God to involve us in talk of the heavenly, pre-existent divine Second Person of the Trinity being born into history 2000 years ago as a human being and bringing with him the full consciousness of his former divinely exalted heavenly existence.

In 1633, a Jesuit theologian Johannes de Lugo, declared that, while Jesus' human body was subject to normal human growth and development, this was not the case in relation to his consciousness. In terms of his mental make-up there was no need for growth or development. The Incarnate Lord was the Eternal Word of God, who already possessed a full and complete or omniscient knowledge of all possible things. This he brought with him from the starry heavens at the time of the Incarnation.

This seemed to suggest that, when the babe of Bethlehem looked up from his lowly manger into the starry eyes of his adoring parents, Joseph and Mary, he already knew, not only all that they knew, but quite literally everything else there was to know because his consciousness was that of the all-knowing, omniscient God.

The problem with this kind of thinking is that it calls into question Jesus' true humanity. It suggests that Jesus is a divine and heavenly being who only *appeared* to be one of us; pretending, as it were, to be subject to all the fears, uncertainties and temptations to which we are subject.

In the late nineteenth century, Anglican theologians such as Bishop Charles Gore of Oxford found this difficult to believe, if not absurd. For one thing, said Gore, it did not take into account those passages in the New Testament which suggest that Jesus' knowledge was the normal, limited knowledge of a typical human being of his day. For Gore, Jesus was really one of us, with limited powers and a restricted self-consciousness. Like us 'he grew in wisdom and stature and in favour with God and Man'. He did not somehow come knowing it all already.

Gore and others therefore spoke of the Incarnation, still in terms of the heavenly pre-existent Divine Person being born as a human person, but acknowledging that the Incarnation involved the abandoning of at least some of the attributes of divinity, or the leaving of them behind in heaven, as it were. Jesus appears to have possessed a residual consciousness *that* he was the Son of the Father, but most of his pre-existent divine attributes such as his omniscience (his all-knowingness) and his omnipotence (his all-powerfulness) were left behind somewhere in the starry heavens when he was born as one of us. Thus, as a human being he possessed limited powers and a limited human mental consciousness; he was a genuine human of his own time and place.

This understanding of things is sometimes alleged to be expressed in the famous passage from Paul's *Epistle to the Philippians*, where he said:

> Let this mind be in you which was in Christ Jesus, who though in the form of God, did not count equality with God a thing to be grasped, or clung on to, but emptied himself, and being found in human form humbled himself, and lived the life of a servant, becoming obedient unto death (2: 5–8).

The trouble with this way of thinking is that it suggests some kind of change in God. *Before* the Incarnation the heavenly Second Person of the Trinity is thought to possess a fully divine consciousness, including a knowledge of all things and all possible divine powers, but *after* the Incarnation that consciousness is said to be significantly different, and his power greatly restricted.

In order to avoid the idea that the Incarnation involved a change in God, still others have spoken, not of the *abandoning* or *self-emptying* of certain divine powers and attributes at the time of the Incarnation, or of leaving them behind in a remote starry heaven, but simply of the *veiling* of the divine behind the outward form of the human. The Divine Person is said to remain unchanged at the Incarnation, but the 'veiling of the flesh' means that only a certain part of his divine mentality and consciousness, along with a specifically limited portion of his powers, can be expressed. Thus he remains unchangeably all-knowing and unrestrictedly all-powerful, but the taking on of a human form entails that only a limited sub-set of these reserve powers can be expressed in the course of his human life. It is like a last generation television set which is only capable of receiving a small portion of what is even now being transmitted.

To take an example from the sporting arena, it is as though a star tennis player is sent on to a tennis court to play tennis with the handicap of wearing a heavy army greatcoat. Underneath he remains unchanged, a tennis player of great prowess, skill and expertise, but many of his abilities and gifts are not brought into play because of the heavy outward clothing of the great coat. So the divine Second Person of the Trinity is imagined at the Incarnation to take on the clothing of humanity. Underneath, hidden as it were, he is God, unchangeably God with unlimited divine powers and attributes, but outwardly he lives and moves in a limited kind of way as a finite human being, as one of us.

In reality, none of these model ways of conceiving how the divine and human come together in the person of the Incarnate Jesus is really satisfactory. For the truth is that the human does not clothe and veil and restrict the full operation of the divine, but just the opposite. The fundamental truth of the Incarnation is not that the humanity conceals and limits the divinity, but rather that it reveals divinity in a unique way that is not available to us anywhere else.

In order to get our thinking right about the Incarnation of God we therefore have to begin, not 'from above' in the starry heavens as it were, with dogmatic talk of the heavenly, pre-existent divine life, but 'from below', from the earthly Jesus as he was humanly experienced, met and known in the historical life he lived 2000 years ago. Instead of thinking of the divinely exalted heavenly Person 'emptying himself' in order to become one of us, we can think of the trappings and powers of divinity as a future possibility which the *human* Jesus, as he lived his earthly life, did not grasp at. In *Philippians* 2 Paul may not be referring to a pre-existent heavenly existence at all. We read that into it. Rather, his point may be that the human Jesus did not seek to possess the kind of power we associate with life on a divine level, but instead emptied himself of that and was content to live a humble human life of the kind exemplified by a slave.

Most of us, whether we are prepared to acknowledge it or not, are concerned with our rights, our position and status. Getting our own way, having power over others in domestic relationships, dominating conversations, making a career out of being on decision-making committees, massaging our egos by getting ourselves into places of importance, making sure others take notice of us or our views – all this is only human. But it is not so with the human Jesus. He did not grasp at divinity as the world conceives of divinity, in terms of possessing great power and control over others. Rather, as he lived his human life, the human Jesus humbled himself, and took on the lowly form of a servant.

Jesus, in other words, though in the form of God, did not live as a star. He did not accede to Satan's temptation to perform extraordinary feats for others to goggle at. He did not come down from the Cross. Still less did he live a life full of show, self-importance, self-interest and self-concern. Rather, he lived in a self-effacing kind of way, in lowly humility and in genuine concern for others.

And it is not that this humble self-effacing form of human life veiled and concealed divinity, but just the opposite. It is the lowly, humble, self-effacing humanity that Jesus assumed, for which he is so poignantly remembered, that *reveals* the true nature of divinity. That is what is really momentous about the

Incarnation. The condescension of the Incarnation is not the choice of the divine to become human but the choice of the human Jesus to live out a particular form of human life unequivocally and steadfastly in love and lowly humility. This is what we call divine.

As revealed in Christ, our God is a God who does what we find it difficult to do. He is by nature a self-effacing God who allows himself to be thought of as nothing, even to the point of being overlooked in his own universe. For God takes the risk, the terrible risk, of allowing us humans to pursue our destiny as responsible persons, with a genuine freedom to respond or not respond to his loving will.

We celebrate today, the 2000th anniversary of the Incarnation, because Jesus Christ, from the lowly circumstances of his birth at Bethlehem to the humiliating circumstances of his rejection and death on the Cross, lived, not as a star performer, but as a servant, and thus reveals the true nature of divinity. Let this mind be in you that was in Christ Jesus. He did not grasp at equality with God, at exercising power and control, but lived a life of concern for others as a lowly servant. If only we could all really make this our own, the world of the new millennium would be a better place.

34

CHOCOLAT

PREACHED IN ST GEORGE'S CATHEDRAL, PERTH
ON EASTER DAY, 15 APRIL 2001.

Last week the Government of Switzerland announced the issue of a new commemorative postage stamp. Normally such an event would not rate a mention in an Australian radio newscast, but this particular postage stamp is attention grabbing. This Swiss postage stamp is different from the ones to which we are accustomed in this country, because it is to be impregnated with a substance which, when handled, gives off the smell of chocolate.

I thought that the newsreader would go on to say that, when the back of this philatelic wonder is licked, ready to be stuck on an envelope, it would also *taste* of chocolate. But, alas, that was not part of the story. The Swiss Government is apparently content for its new postage stamp simply to *smell* of chocolate, a smell which issues through little pores in the paper when it is touched.

The issue of this stamp last week is timed, not as you might think, to coincide with Easter, with its supply of chocolate

Easter eggs and chocolate Easter Bunnies; but rather, this chocolate-smelling postage stamp is being issued simply to commemorate the centenary of the industry of Swiss chocolate making.

You might be forgiven, however, for anticipating a link with Easter, for chocolate has certainly become a part of Easter celebrations in our society. Chocolate eggs are to Easter as Christmas pudding is to Christmas. It is not, therefore, a surprise to find that the film *Chocolat*, which has been recently showing in the cinemas, has a religious theme – a theme that focuses our attention on Lent and Easter. Indeed, if the scenes of movies could be accompanied by appropriate smells, our movie theatres would have been heavy with the sweet smell of chocolate.

In the film, set in the late 1950s, the heroine Vianne, an apparently unmarried mother played by Juliette Binoche, comes into a French village with her small daughter and sets up a chocolaterie. She rents a broken-down and deserted old shop and transforms it into a place of delicious surprises. But she is apparently insensitive to the fact that her new business enterprise is being launched smack in the middle of Lent. The local Mayor, who calls all the shots, urges the people to avoid the chocolaterie. As a kind of church warden he edits the local parish priest's sermons, and directs him to denounce the chocolate maker from the pulpit.

Believe it or not, this film was also condemned in real life from the pulpits of North America by the Roman Catholic Bishops' Conference, which judged the film to be 'morally offensive', apparently for promoting an irreverent approach to the keeping of Lent, and for making light of the Church's teaching and discipline.

One suspects this heavy handed action was prompted by more than the possibility that Juliette Binoche's character,

Vianne, might be an undesirable role model for the local North American population. For there has been a longstanding suspicion of chocolate in sections of the Church for many centuries. Indeed, once a Pope actually banned Jesuits from eating chocolate, not just in Lent, but at any time of the year, because he believed that chocolate was an aphrodisiac.

The idea that chocolate is to be avoided as a temptation to sin, and not just the sin of gluttony, probably conditions the sense of alarm felt by the Mayor when confronted by the establishment of the chocolaterie in the middle of the village, by an attractive woman with a child but without a male partner, and in Lent to boot. Somehow the chocolate is a token of something a little more sinister than you might at first think.

I happened to see this film on an aeroplane, and I must confess that I thoroughly enjoyed it. If we do not allow our Christian sensibilities to be too threatened by it, we can appreciate the film's warm humanity, and its gentle charm.

Our enjoyment should abound even more when it dawns upon us that, from a Christian point of view, the chocolaterie actually makes a positive community-building contribution to the life of the village. The quality of local human belonging in one bundle of village life is transformed by the chocolaterie. A slightly grumpy and surly grandmother, played by Judi Dench, is reconnected with her grandson, and through him with her own estranged daughter. Others, a widower and a widow, are brought together unexpectedly in a new and life-giving relationship of love. A battered and abused wife finds the strength to free herself from her domestic oppression. The villagers work through and beyond the domineering, alienating influence of the Mayor in their lives, to assert themselves and to take charge of their own destiny. And at the end of the film, the Mayor himself melts with a smile, as the whole village enters joyfully into the Easter celebrations, sharing chocolates all around in street festivities outside church.

At the end of the day chocolate, potentially the cause of social division in the village, becomes the outward and visible sign, a kind of sacrament, of the inward and spiritual grace of renewed togetherness in community. An Easter miracle has occurred.

When you think about it, this is how our exchange of chocolate Easter eggs should be for us, bringing together members of families, grandparents and children, the isolated and alone, as friends together in a human community of shared happiness.

In our culture, at any time of the year, chocolates provide us with a regularly preferred kind of gift. When made into a gift they become something more than just a material thing; they begin by grace to transmit life-giving spiritual realities. When a box of chocolates is taken from the shelf of a local chocolaterie, it begins to take on a new significance which distinguishes those particular chocolates from all the chocolates that are left behind on the shelf in the store. These specific chocolates, once they are purchased for a specific purpose, and taken home and carefully wrapped, and then brought within an interpersonal relationship when they are presented as a gift by a lover to his beloved, bear a new meaning and significance. They are more than a sign of the lover's love. The chocolates actually convey the reality of his love to the beloved. Without them, or some other token similar to them, the beloved might find herself wondering if she was really loved at all. My wife Ann tells me that she actually kept the box, long after my first gift of chocolates to her were eaten, and even the wrapping paper; this box of chocolates was a token of love with a lingering effect.

At some restaurants there is a dessert known as 'Death by Chocolate'; in fact, chocolate is more often than not a token of new life and of self-gift – love.

Now, the bread and the wine of the eucharist is the same for us. When particular bread and wine is taken and separated out from other bread and wine and brought within a set of community relationships, it is consecrated for a sacred purpose. That is what consecration means – setting apart. Its significance for us Christians is that it becomes transformed; as a gift over which we give thanks, it conveys to us the life-giving spiritual reality of the love of God. It bears the stamp of love. Indeed, the sharing of bread and wine brings with it the aroma of the love of God as we handle it, and we are all drawn together, in the mystery of being drawn closer to him.

Easter is the event of the building of new community out of the dispirited band of Jesus' fragmented and dispersed followers. It was in their re-gathering in the welcoming, forgiving presence of the one they had betrayed and left to die alone upon the Cross, that they knew his love, living still, in the breaking and sharing of bread.

An Easter miracle also happens amongst us when we are called out of our isolation into warm and loving human community. This is an anticipation of our hope for all men and women of every race and nation in the entire world. Our prayer is that even the homeless and the desperately hungry will one day enjoy the chocolate of life and the aroma of the love of God.

In other words, what happens amongst us on the scale of a local village, is a token of what is possible in the global village. The possibility of the renewal of human community life is not just an idle dream, for we taste it already; it is something that we know is possible for humankind because we know it in an anticipated kind of way actually coming to be amongst us. That is an Easter miracle; and it grounds our hope of more to come.

As we look upon the world we cannot avoid the stark reality of its fragmentation and tension. The standoff between China and America over a downed spy plane has grabbed the headlines. We reacted with concern as British farmers watched helplessly as their lives fell apart because of the ravages of foot and mouth disease. One day we will understand more fully the cause of this disaster in the commitment of our age to economic rationalism. Once local British farmers sent their stock to local abattoirs. Today shipments of pigs go from Britain to Holland and vice versa, as people chase a better price. It was only a matter of time before the spread of disease across Europe followed in the wake of the chase for more money.

In Africa whole communities face extinction because of the ravages of HIV/AIDS. Across the world there are now more than 34 million people living with HIV/AIDS. In some places the Church struggles to educate the young in safe practices, while at the same time some drug companies deny already infected parents access to affordable life-saving drugs. We understand the companies' desire to maximise their profit; but when people are desperate and dying it is morally very questionable. Elsewhere, unpayable Third World debt is so crippling that children are denied an education, and health services, while others of us in the world enjoy the chocolates of life. What a completely hopeless spectacle!

But even in the face of all this we do not lose hope. We do not lose hope because we know something of the miracle of the enjoyment of new life together in community, which is the promise, the first dividend, of a greater yield to come, not just for us but for all men and women. The Church is that part of the world where the Kingdom of God is dawning as people align their lives with the good purposes of God.

That is why Easter has meaning not just for us but for the whole world. It is the advance publicity of greater attractions to come. Its celebration is not just a matter of overindulgence, chocolate Easter eggs to the point of death by chocolate; rather, it is the sharing of what makes life so wondrously enjoyable for us, and the promise of a greater outpouring of good things to come for all God's people. The Easter renewal of our faith commitment, the renewal of our baptismal vows, the re-entry into community life renewed in the Spirit with the aroma of love, is what alone gives us the strength to press on with our mission to put God's stamp upon the world.